The Architect:
Four Countries
Four Faces
I

Marga Jann, DPUC, RIBA, AIA

ArrowGate

Published by Arrow Gate Publishing Ltd 2019

15 14 13 12 11 10 9 8 7 6

A CIP catalogue record for this book is available from the British Library.
ISBN 978-1-913142-04-9
eBook 978-1-913142-05-6

Arrow Gate Publishing 85, Great Portland Street, London W1W 7LT

Visit www.arrowgatepublishing.com to read more about our books and to buy them. You will also find articles, author interviews, writing tips and news of any author events, and you can sign up for our e-newsletters so that you're always first to read about our new releases.

For my children

*'Oh, that you would bless me indeed, and enlarge my territory,
that Your hand would be with me, and that You would keep me
from evil, that I may not cause pain.'*

–1 CHRONICLES 4 10 NKJV

Some of the narratives in this trilogy are true, some are
hypothetical, and some are allusion or illusion—often names
and places are changed to protect those involved

•   1   •

Cambridge, 2005

IT TOOK A WHILE for the garrulous Porter to notice the stealthy figure in the upper left-hand security monitor while we chatted about the forthcoming conference on architectural education. The monochromatic image included a view of my ivy-covered Cambridge College outer door, the lock of which the dark figure in the monitor was toying with far too deftly.

The seamless black silhouette was indubitably that of a tallish woman in an abaya and hijab.

I had suspected someone had been watching and pursuing me for some time (beyond the omnipresent internet and 'security camera' surveillance) —I had learned too much and the professorial research I was writing up, benign though it was, had recently gone online (see the articles at the end of this tome).

Also, I was an espousing non-violent Quaker Christian teaching architecture in fundamentalist Muslim arenas (which included hostile Saudi Arabia) where I had previously been targeted as a persona non-grata. Though I sensed an imminent accounting, I nonetheless expected my discovery to take longer. Below is my narrative; I leave it to the reader to determine why, apart from the obvious faith issues, anyone might be remotely interested in me.

Sri Lanka

As an architect and Fulbright scholar to Sri Lanka after the 2004 tsunami, I did not expect to walk into and unwittingly uncover a criminal arena involving international drug and arms trade, misappropriation of relief funds, pervasive computer hacking, extensive money laundering, terrorism, and trafficking linked to hidden academic and political agendas.

The only transgression missing was murder, and that could now follow soon enough. My teaching and research were to take me to lecture halls as far afield as Korea,

Cyprus, and Uganda— where I acquired significant Islamic shadows—both extreme and hermetic.

I write from the relative security of my self-styled 'safe house' as a Visiting Fellow at the University of Cambridge—fertile recruiting ground for MI5 in tandem to its wider and better-known academic mission, where no one would have expected a mature, scholarly architect and professor to be up to anything more than 'pedestrian'. Indeed, Lucy Cavendish College, my home base, was founded to support the studies and research of 'mature women' and as such had a reputation for being seriously and uniquely academic.

I expected the air to be hot and humid upon my arrival in Sri Lanka, but even my research stint in Delhi, India as a Swarthmore College undergrad did not prepare me for the sweltering wave of heat that slapped me harshly as I walked off the plane. After a brief adjustment period (and over 30 mosquito bites during my first night in dengue-infested Colombo), I began my design teaching stint with a focus on disaster-relief housing. The Fulbright Commission was located down the street from the office of a Cambridge colleague who put me in touch with the Architecture Department at the University of Moratuwa, and I soon found myself teaching at both U Moratuwa and the Colombo School of Architecture. But it wasn't until I started working 'in the field' as an architect that huge NGO (Non-Governmental Organisation) anomalies began to surface, and moral dilemmas confronted me on what seemed an almost daily basis.

There had been twenty-six different branches of the Red Cross from at least as many countries working in Sri Lanka at that time, mostly disorganised and largely stepping on each other's toes. The scope of the tsunami disaster was such that NGO workers immediately flew in with little planning or preparation. People donated with excellent intentions but gave little consideration to whom or what precisely they were giving, and churches sent missionaries and individual 'do-gooders' without 'thinking things through'—e.g. blankets and crates of bottled water were delivered to a tropical country with oppressive year-round heat and huge stockpiles of mineral water. In many ways, this 'knee-jerk' reaction added to the chaos more than to the aid effort. Furthermore, NGO websites provided clear directives as to how to make donations, but none offered counsel or help to the tens of thou-sands in need.

The Head of the Sri Lankan Red Cross, for one, had told me that $500,000,000 received in relief aid would not be available for 'short-term reconstruction' although the design work my students and I had produced was 'greatly appreciated'. The director and his abaya-clad assistant explained that the funds had been 'put aside' at a high-interest rate in Switzerland for 'long-term development'. As a colleague wrote to me in her email of 8 August 2014, 'All is well here in Sri Lanka. The country is changing fast with new roads, sidewalks, parks and buildings every-where. It is nice to see...' And another colleague mentioned in an email of 6 September 2014: 'A lot of international projects are under construction. You will see a big change in the urban fabric of Colombo and some of the other cities. An improvement to the builtscape I must say.' So, though these Red Cross donations did not go towards immediate tsunami relief and reconstruction as intended, on an encouraging note much funding appears to have gone into long-term development as opposed to permanent deep private pockets.

Despite the colossal amount of capital pouring into the island, trying to find backing to construct our pro-bono, sustainably designed disaster-relief shelters for the vast destitute of post-tsunami Sri Lanka was almost like trying to find a needle in a haystack.

Habitat for Humanity and the Colombo Scots Kirk (Church) were the only entities to show true interest in our design work—enough to provide the incentive we needed to continue with our small reconstruction effort, and which unwittingly led to intense involvement with the Tamil Tiger controlled North and Pakistani refugee community.

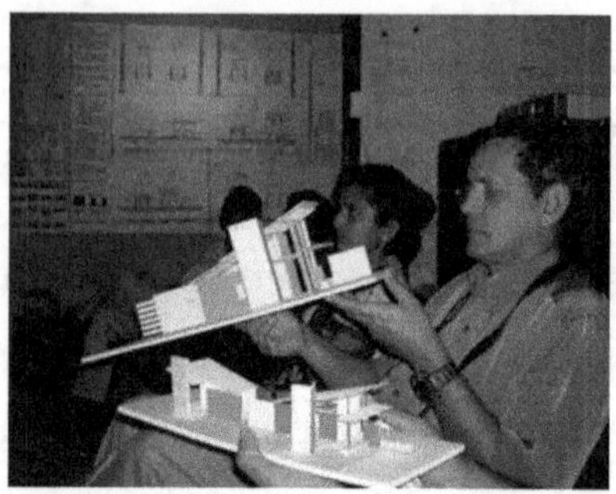

Sri Lankan student work (prototypical disaster relief housing) presentation to Habitat for Humanity

The Scots Kirk was a popular meeting place for expats who were there not just for its spiritual dimension but for many other forms of sanctuary—many were refugees fleeing persecution on their home front. A Pakistani Anglican pastor claimed to know where Osama Bin Laden was, and it was generally understood by the entire Pakistani community that Bin Laden was incontestably in Pakistan with the US government naively and unknowingly 'paying' President Musharraf to protect him. The wife of a Pakistani ambassador I had met in my travels inadvertently confirmed this conviction.

Shortly after settling in Colombo, I was sent to Islamabad by the United States Government as a regional Fulbright specialist following the 2005 earthquake which had just devastated the northern region of Pakistan. I was invited to give talks there on our tsunami-related design work in Sri Lanka to a group of Fulbright scholars who had also been posted to South Asia, as well as on earthquake reconstruction to numerous Pakistani officials outlining our 'live project' methodology (designs for real clients which have the potential of getting built)—which, by the way, has largely since been adopted and implemented by Pakistani 'starchitects' such as Yasmeen Lari. In one of my audiences, I noticed a figure entirely veiled in black—attire not uncommon for Pakistan but not typical indigenous garb either—she was unsettlingly sitting in the front row assiduously taking notes and filming my talk.

Traversing the airport in Karachi had been tortuous as I was the only woman there except for four nuns who became my 'security blanket' and to whom I stuck like glue; I subsequently heard in the local news that terrorists had killed those four nuns and the story shattered me. A short while later, a talented and gracious British-Australian architect and collaborator I'd met and worked with in Uganda, Ross Langdon, and his eight-month pregnant fiancé were brutally shot in the Nairobi Westgate Shopping Centre attack, dying within minutes. Terrorism is often much closer to us than we think, planning and plotting as we soundly sleep unawares in our beds.

Amidst this tumultuous backdrop, the studio and design initiatives my students and I undertook provided a haven of serenity. Through my studios I got to know the culture of Sri Lanka (and the other places I have lived and worked in) intimately, making lasting friendships now nurtured by Facebook, related social media, and subsequent visits.

Only one per cent of the Sri Lankan population receives a university education; hence my students were truly exceptional and produced remarkable work.

Not long after I arrived in Colombo, through a weekly NGO forum/coordination meeting, I met Norwegian architect, Pål Kavli, who worked for NGO FORUT and was one of the few other western architects on the island engaged in tsunami-related reconstruction, as most involved were engineers. Pål joined me in our studio from time-to-time, and we attempted to organise a 'live' residential village project with FORUT in the Tamil Tiger controlled North as a peace-making mission employing design for social change.

FORUT was one of the few NGO's committed to assisting in the north; the Norwegians have historically played an important role there as regional peacemaker/arbitrator.

But the morning of our site visit, which we had planned for weeks, a group of downcast students awaited us outside the architecture school. Their parents, fearful for their safety, had obliged them to forego the trip at the last minute—and in retrospect, wisely—that afternoon a well-known writer and acquaintance from the Colombo Book Club, Nihal De Silva, was killed in a landmine explosion while crossing the Wilpattu National Park up north along a route we had planned to take. The whole world seemed a metaphorical, if not very real, minefield at that time.

As an architect I caught a glimpse of what happened (or didn't happen) to many 'relief funds'—some of which went to absurdly high NGO salaries and perks—like up-market housing, abundant household help, private school fees and chauffeured transportation. While it is expected that 30-40% of donations are legitimately intended to cover NGO overhead, and despite the low cost of living in Sri Lanka, it is reasonable to suggest that the figure was more like 70-90% in many instances, although certainly not all NGO's were so 'generous' to their staff in 'hardship' posts. Direct donation to individuals in need, where possible, always ensures safe delivery. But large-scale projects require management, and management incurs a cost—the question is how much cost.

In the face of corruption and 'irregularity', it is hard to know how best to be impactful or to react—whether to exercise 'restraint of tongue and pen' (turn a blind eye or be fired if not executed in some arenas), or to confront—keeping in mind that through non-action, one can easily become participatory. While doing nothing can be perceived as the safer, more comfortable avenue and often more conducive to job security, it is not by any means the more ethical. I felt somewhat powerless at that juncture, often reflecting on that well-known AA prayer by Reinhold Niebuhr:

> God grant me the serenity
> to accept the things, I cannot change; courage to change the
> things I can; and wisdom to know the difference.

Short of a seared conscience, it can be psychologically difficult (and certainly was for me) to ignore abuse of power and funds. While walking past a seriously injured person in the street and doing nothing would be, by common standards of morality, highly uncaring and unethical (the French would designate such behaviour as criminal or 'non-assistance à personne endanger'), walking past an illegally parked car would ordinarily be inconsequential, requiring action only from the appropriate authorities.

So, the dilemma seemed to involve a question of degree as well as context.

I believe that the threads of malevolence I have encountered in my travels and related practice, teaching and research (much in the developing world) warrant attention, in the hope (naïve, perhaps) that exposure and accountability will curb misdeed.

As Albert Einstein said, *'the world is a dangerous place to live, not because of the people who are evil, but because of the people who don't do anything about it.'* [1]

'Whistle-blowing' however can and has proven to be dangerous, as this narrative will demonstrate.

After my stint in Sri Lanka (I had spent the prior six years between Stanford and Paris), I tried my hand teaching at a self-proclaimed 'Christian' university in the mid-west of the United States, only to find myself extremely let down by the rampant provincialism and in-fighting. I have learned that branding and marketing do not necessarily accurately reflect content and praxis by any means. Concurrent to the realisation that I was apparently not going to be an asset in the ways the university had anticipated and the venue was not going to provide the spiritual connection and fellowship I need-ed, a job offer materialised at Duksung U in South Korea (which I was to affiliate to U Hawaii), building on my Fulbright 'live project' work. Spiritual warfare ('the Christian concept of taking a stand against supernatural

---

[1] http://www.goodreads.com/quotes/tag/evil last accessed 13 August 2014.

evil forces')[2], seemingly within the Christian university, intensified. Additionally, and very oddly, a few visitors wrapped in seamless black cloaks showed up at some of my lectures and disappeared before I could catch or chat with them—perturbing, though not preoccupying. In retrospect, I had indubitably ignored serious warning signs.

My architecture students and I in mid-west America developed and designed a large tsunami village for Hindu widows south of Chennai, India, which is now under construction, albeit not faithfully to the plans we had meticulously drawn up despite constant interlocution with the client, troublesome when one thinks how the time, attention and effort might have been more effectively and 'sustainably' deployed.

Concurrently and per a fairly common modus operandi, the more success I seemed to have in the design studio with students, the more potential flak or envy I seemed to elicit from colleagues and administrators (with little or no teaching to do).

The pattern has proven reliable over the years—ostensibly beyond the usual academic politics. When my evaluations were excellent, resentment was palpable—

---

[2] http://en.wikipedia.org/wiki/Spiritual_warfare last accessed 13 August 2014.

when they were less than stellar, I was held to account; it was a no-win situation.

As Bette Midler has said, *'The worst part of success is trying to find someone who is happy for you.'* [3]

Of course, I did make some dear and close friends—mature and accomplished colleagues (some who became collaborators) involved in their own fascinating projects and research—who provided much-appreciated support and expertise. It should be noted that many of our 'live projects' were direct or indirect charitable 'missions' projects and as such attracted negative attention on the spiritual plane, drawing us into the usual treacherous battlefield of divergent public opinion, jealousy, and sometimes wilful sabotage.

A question often asked was, 'How do you get these projects?'— easy to answer as paucity is rampant the world over; one only has to be willing to 'make poverty history' (Oxfam).

I would be remiss not to mention, before moving on, a tragic phenomenon revealed with the wreckage of the tsunami throughout South Asia: the trafficking and sexual abuse of children (an ongoing and horrendously

---

[3] http://www.goodreads.com/quotes/tag/jealousy last accessed 2 October 2014.

widespread phenomenon which encompasses areas as 'sophisticated' as Cambridge today).

One has only to 'google' 'child trafficking tsunami' for endless heart-breaking tales, for instance:

South Asia: U.S. "horrified" at child trafficking in tsunami aftermath

http://reliefweb.int/report/indonesia/south-asia-us-horrified-child-trafficking-tsunami-aftermath

DISPLACED WOMEN AND CHILDREN TSUNAMI SURVIVORS NEED IMMEDIATE PROTECTION FROM TRAFFICKING AND ABUSE

HTTP://WWW.WOMENSREFUGEECOMMISSION.ORG/PRESS-ROOM/409-DISPLACED-WOMEN-AND-CHILDREN- TSUNAMI-SURVIVORS-NEED-IMMEDIATE-PROTECTION-FROM-TRAFFICKING-AND-ABUSE

The sexual abuse, commercial sexual exploitation and trafficking of children in Sri Lanka. Sri Lanka Research Report

http://resourcecentre.savethechildren.se/library/sexual-abuse-commercial-sexual-exploitation-and-trafficking-children-sri-lanka-sri-lanka

No words suffice to describe the cruelty and horrendous implications of trafficking. Of minimal consolation is Mahatma Gandhi's reflection: *When I despair, I remember that all through history the way of truth and love has always won. There have been tyrants and murderers, and for a time, they can seem invincible, but in the end, they always fall. Think of it—always.'* [4]

In many respects, the Cambridge Wolfson Visiting Fellows' house, where I was a member, had become a hub of counter-terrorist activism. While women are unlikely participants in this arena, the fierce Tamil Tiger women soldiers (original suicide-bombers) and growing feminine jihadist population at the larger international (ISIS) level warranted, to my view, some sort of counter-commitment besides deep concern. Being non-participatory while 'in the field' was out of the question. Whenever I thought I'd 'take a break' and retire into sedentary, routine academe or practice, the history of the four nuns would haunt me and confirm that neutrality was no option—an attribute I reproach in many of my colleagues, who seem largely to perpetuate denial regarding world affairs, spirituality, death and the 'after-life.' I suppose, too, that having clients and friends involved in national security and government, it was inevitable that I adopt some of their interest.

But it was with Tony, engaged in rescuing abused children and women, as well as serving as the director of

---

[4]http://www.goodreads.com/quotes/tag/evil last accessed 13 August 2014.

Habitat for Humanity Sri Lanka, that I actually took some risk and ventured forth into the isolated north of the island—despite repeated warnings from the US Embassy and Fulbright Commission, and independent of my academic work. When we arrived at the 'border' in Habitat's well-travelled van, several Tamil Tiger soldiers jumped aboard brandishing ominous looking weapons. We had an infant in our crew of seven which proved an effective common denominator. The Tigers seemed quite happy that I was in tow (as I had been warned) and wanted to take pictures with me (which I cautiously refused). Once we got our official-looking letter stamped with the Tiger insignia, we proceeded onwards to the devastated northern beaches. NGO's generally didn't make it this far, and the situation was truly appalling. While Habitat was considered Christian, as were my companions, the Tigers didn't appear to mind at all what faith we represented—help would clearly be appreciated wherever it came from. Tony was a constant reminder of the Quaker adage, 'Let your life speak'.

Habitat was, for him, a kind of 'front' for out-reach which afforded unrestricted access to the abused and destitute. He often said his work was, on many levels, very dangerous. Travelling with him and his team I learned, among other things, that the abused also become abusers, and the resulting vicious cycle can be extremely difficult to break.

The crew spent the night at a pastor's home (missionaries in the Tamil-controlled north, which at the time was not dissimilar to operating in ISIS-controlled territory), awaiting an accountant who was to arrive from Bangkok to review Habitat's financial records, which he did yearly. Due to problems at the border, Peter sadly missed a lavish Sri Lankan welcome breakfast prepared for him days in advance. When he finally did turn up (a few days late), he arrived fashionably dressed in safari gear (the fare worn mostly by those who glamorize safari treks and remote expeditions)—a kind, handsome, ginger-haired man whom I was to see again very briefly, like ships passing in the night, as a tourist with my children and grandchildren in Bangkok some years later.

Apart from a few Tamil-backed NGO's and FORUT, Habitat for Humanity was probably the only significant international organisation involved in reconstruction in the Sri Lankan north. Tony couldn't build from our designs unfortunately due to what he called 'equity issues'—i.e. Habitat had already built hundreds of 'cookie-cutter' homes; if the group built from our 'up-market' designs, though similar in cost to the homes under construction, envy and social tension were likely to ensue. In a conflict-ridden zone, any further antagonism was to be mitigated, so Habitat insisted on treating everybody equally or 'equitably', and design was an important consideration. We had arrived on the scene a little too late.

Tsunami victims living under black plastic garbage bags (whose lack of security encouraged rampant abuse, although their isolation protected them from that of the southern tourists) were, of course, grateful for Habitat 'cookie-cutter' homes—a luxury in comparison to their make-shift 'tents' with their lack of sanitation outside of the beach. The 'mujahedin' Hindu Tigers were growing increasingly and wretchedly poor and desperate. Was Habitat's message of hope and charity connecting with them at all, we wondered? The full-fledged war that eventually broke out on the island preempted any peaceful north-south settlement, bringing further devastation, exploitation, and widespread abuse, including rampant torture. The Muslim population in the region, though a minority compared to the Hindu Tamil presence, suffered similarly. The Muslims were by-and-large fairly radical, and on a ferry crossing home, I felt like I might as well have been in Saudi Arabia given the number of women on board heavily clad in black, wearing gloves and face veils in the sweltering Sri Lankan heat.

The rest of the year progressed relatively benignly, whatever that implied. At the airport in Chennai returning from a visit to our 'widows' village' construction site, I was followed by a persistent Indian woman recording my every move in a video with her phone, and whom I only managed to lose after about ten minutes. She wore a light-coloured floral sari and had audaciously pursued me into the ladies' room, where I had attempted to vanish to no avail; only confrontation and a threat to call the security guards turned her away. It wasn't your average teaching year, but I wouldn't have traded it for anything. I was sad not to be able to go back north and do more than a visit, however.

•　　2　　•

Korea

HOPING FOR SOME MUCH-NEEDED 'downtime' given my anticipated nine contact hour/week teaching schedule in Seoul, and looking forward to respite from the ravages of 'extreme climate destabilization', war and more recently, the stint in the mid-west U.S. at Judson U, I headed to Korea via Cambridge, rapidly learning en route that 'spiritual warfare' has no geographical boundaries—though one could argue that 'principalities and powers' do. I sat next to a woman completely veiled in black, and who remained so, for the entire duration of my flight. And though I was to teach in an Interior Design department, I arrived at a filthy and dilapidated apartment with the barest minimum of furniture—a lopsided swivel chair, a single bed that reeked of cigarette smoke, and an ancient metal desk. The apartment itself, however, was architect-designed and gave onto a delightful garden from which I could watch the seasons turn. I had warm ex-pat neighbours, a tax-free salary, and distinguished colleagues. It only took a week or two to get the apartment into shape, and I soon discovered there was a French bakery around the corner, and I had only a brisk, enjoyable ten-minute walk to school.

Though there were some minor language difficulties and cultural misunderstandings as might be expected (described in the academic articles at the end of this book), tribulation really began when I took a 'tourist trip' to North Korea. On the bus were two self-proclaimed 'spies'—one from the Italian Embassy in Seoul who was vetting a post as Italian Ambassador to Pyongyang, and another, more discreet traveller, claimed to be a news reporter/photographer who kindly showed us all how to hide digital photographs on our cameras and cell phones (these devices were systematically checked for 'unauthorised' photography at the border upon exit). Much of my everyday routine (again, described in greater detail at the end of this book) was what might be anticipated by any visiting university professor in an 'exotic,' cross-cultural setting.

The internationally engaged architect's itinerant profession, in tandem with evermore peripatetic teaching venues, provides unparalleled mobility and access, and many of us indubitably have the makings of first-rate moles. Indeed, much of the information recounted herewith would never have been accessible via satellite or computer monitoring, from hacking to 'remote desktop' surveillance, or even official on-the-ground 'smoke and mirror' operations.

It often seemed I was often just in the right (or wrong) place at the right or wrong time—spiritual 'serendipity' one might say. Travelling to North Korea was extremely painful (and reminiscent of Moscow during the Cold War thirty years or so earlier) in that we were obliged to patiently sit on a cold bus in a parking lot at the border for hours before the North Korean officials allowed us to proceed. We were led and followed at a snail's pace by vehicular escorts for the entire duration of our journey, which we had hoped would be a stress-free, enjoyable visit.

Despite our tour being restricted to well-maintained historic sites, North Korea appeared extremely poor.

Everyone we saw on the street wore traditional white and blue indigenous garb, almost a kind of uniform. Once we finally made it across the border, everything had seemed to go relatively smoothly—for the first few hours.

We bought postcards which showed North Korean propaganda (nothing else was available) at a state-run tourist shop. We mailed them off with bright red stamps and benign inscriptions (knowing they would be scrutinised) like 'Wish you were here' or 'You don't know what you're missing!' or 'Miss you terribly, Happy Birthday' which made us all laugh (since our inscriptions were tongue-in-cheek)—laughter which, however, set off a chain of unfortunate events which quickly made us realise just how tenuous our situation was.

Our uninhibited amusement made the guards not only curious but highly suspicious, thinking we were undoubtedly laughing at them or at some offhand slur about North Korean culture. Our 'escorts' chose to interrogate the young-looking Italian (future 'Italian ambassador' who elected to remain anonymous vis-à-vis his inquisitors). They asked to see his passport, which was ordinary enough and checked his visa—apparently a tourist visa similar to ours. Then they took him to a room apart, and we did not see or hear of him further for what seemed an eternity.

Long, uncertain waiting appears to be a favourite chastisement for victims of controlling tyrants, and joy and complicity appear poorly tolerated by the oppressor in the oppressed. When the 'Italian ambassador' reappeared after several further tedious hours, he told us he had spent most of his time indeed waiting, like us, albeit in silence in a dark room. He further related that he was thankfully not obliged to divulge his true identity, and when asked briefly by the North Korean guards what the laughter was all about, through the 'art of diplomacy' he apparently managed to appease his interlocutors with a commentary about his broken diet given the superb quality of the North Korean lunch—and by now everyone had learned not to laugh. Three months earlier two wandering tourists had been detained and imprisoned, and we certainly had no intention of following suit. It took just over a month for my family in Hawaii to receive the postcards which they tell me are treasured to this day.

We had an understandably difficult time enjoying the rest of our trip, as our 'hosts' had no doubt intended, and the ride back to Seoul felt long and harrowing despite the relatively short distance. Once safely back on familiar turf, I turned to the design of a large, expansive plaza for the Seoul National Museum of History and thought little more about the North Korean experience. Over the years architecture has proven a wonderful distraction from the woes of the world—although it indubitably has some of its own. I picked up a renovation project for the U.S. Embassy in Seoul as well, involving my design students at Duksung in both endeavours. The Embassy, at six storeys originally the tallest building in Seoul, was now a shabby, dilapidated pile and the U.S. government had been looking for a site for a new complex for over forty years. At the time of writing things look hopeful—a previous site upon which construction had begun revealed archaeological treasures below grade as soon as excavation started, and work was halted at the insistence of the Korean government though $13,000,000 had already been spent by the U.S. (taxpayer), never to be reimbursed. Plans for a new complex have been in the pipeline for years, with a new site (a section of property on United States Forces Korea's Camp Coiner—i.e. an existing US military base) identified in 2011.

Interestingly, students seem to prefer working on high-end projects like embassies or dream houses to orphanages and tsunami villages for the destitute (for which design challenges can be far greater and more thought-provoking).

So, I try to prescribe a healthy mix, delegating the bulk of 'live projects' to professional practice since student work can sometimes be too amateurish to present to the less compassionate client.

But for pro-bono charity work, the paradigm makes good sense, with clients sometimes requested to contribute small donations according to their ability to the university towards scholarships, field trip expenses, books, or similar. Students get early hands-on internship experience through the model and are typically encouraged to work together collaboratively.

An Oxbridge alumni dinner brought me to the Seoul U.K. ambassador's residence for a networking event where I was introduced to a former Korean ambassador to Washington, and in the course of the evening, I casually related the North Korean incident, which appeared to have special meaning for Ambassador Lee Joon—because, as he explained, to his knowledge no future Italian embassy (or ambassador) had been planned for Pyong-yang!

So, if it was indeed true that no 'future Italian ambassador' was in the pipeline for Pyong-yang, Fabrizio's pretence had just become baffling. As I was leaving the stately residence, a server in a black turban and hanbok (the native, loose-fitting Korean dress) bumped into me apologetically, smiled and took my picture. Clumsy surveillance, I told myself. Or paranoia? Like thinking, we were all being spied on until Snowden broke the news that in fact, we were.

The next day I called the Italian Embassy in Seoul—it was no surprise that Fabrizio Giacometti, as his name read on the gilded Embassy calling card, was unknown to the switchboard operator there. Many nations are watching North Korea, and I guess intrigue is to be expected in this part of the world. I have come to realise that the unification of divided nations (or cities) is typically unlikely in that a host of jobs have to be lost on 'one side of the fence' to enable a merger (among other complex issues)—often leading to a war, as in Sri Lanka. In Cyprus, unification talks are generally perceived as a charade, and the talks to date have kept both north and south side 'leadership' employed for over forty years. As man struggles for survival, his natural tendency seems to be competitive rather than collaborative. It has been my experience that collaboration is a far more effective and rewarding m.o., both practically and psychologically, but collaboration takes wisdom, experience, willingness, compromise and maturity to both initiate and cultivate. I pushed the puzzle of Fabrizio to the back of my mind.

Old Seoul is a rabbit's warren of narrow cobblestone lanes and historic tiled-roof Korean houses, mostly well-preserved and often renovated in 'upmarket' fashion around trendy commercial nodes these days—and the perfect place for a James Bond chase, which a small group of emerging 'shadows' in black seemed to appreciate wholly. As I cautiously strolled down the steep incline of the old town's central spine admiring its architecture and the stunning views of modern Seoul, a local resident stepped out of his house, revealing a rich traditional interior. As I strained to peek inside, the man kindly asked if I would like to visit—an irresistible offer for an ever-inquisitive architect—and seemingly providing some potential crisis intervention. The tight courtyard was bordered by a tapered wooden veranda linking the various contiguous rooms and their sliding wooden doors around a well-manicured, pristine archetypal Korean garden. The colourful garden was further flanked by a few large terracotta pots which would historically have

served for refrigeration. As I slid one of the doors open to explore the house itself, I interrupted a tea ceremony: four figures, seemingly women in black abayas, sat on the floor and motioned to me to join them. The dreamlike improbability of the situation yielded a jolt. The man who had opened the door extending the invitation was now, shockingly, trying to block the door—but somehow, I managed to push through him and promptly bolted into the street. Given the stature and build of those who now trailed me, it seemed likely that they were not women, but men dressed in feminine Islamic garb.

As I ran, I felt evil adrift—like the tip of a great, bottomless iceberg. This old Seoul set-up implied alarming tracking capability, particularly as I was not carrying my cell phone with me. I had sent an email to a friend earlier mentioning I was going for a stroll in the old quarter but had not indicated anything else. As I glanced back, there was no longer a vague party in black chasing me but a whole gang of Asian-looking men, so my intuition in that respect had been correct. I could not imagine what their interest in an architecture professor could be. With limited time for further reflection, I ran as if in a high-stake marathon.

My principal and initial experience with Islam had been a startling encounter year earlier at Parsons School of Design in Paris, where I had had some delightful Saudi architecture students. Through them, I had met an array of interesting Saudi characters including Bin Mahfouz, Al-Hejailan and Bin Laden family members—but I could not through them establish or make any connection to the events unfolding here. My mind raced.

A Pakistani-French filmmaker who had lost no time in introducing me briefly to the strange world of purdah and domestic violence came to mind. But since becoming a Christian, my main Pakistani friends were Christians in Sri Lanka fleeing persecution on their home front. It was impossible to connect the dots.

By now, though running downhill at a gazelle's pace, I could hear loud footsteps close behind. This chase was no game. What had I done to warrant such adversaries? Suddenly I caught a taxi in my peripheral vision dropping someone off in an alleyway to the right; I ran to the car and escaped by a hair with a fist pounding on a locked window and my heart thumping heavily. Dusk had started to fall and a flurry of glowing red roof-top neon crosses illuminating Seoul's churches reminded me of an ever-present Divine hand. My pursuers would not have related to the salvation and hope the red neon crosses represented—their witlessness the only reason I could imagine at the time for their pursuit.

It seemed unlikely that my colleagues, friends, and even the police would have believed my narrative, so foolishly, perhaps, I did not relate the incident immediately. I felt I needed to 'regroup' fast and first; I still had a semester of teaching to complete and felt 'stuck' in Seoul for a while. While there was no obvious link to any-thing that had happened in North Korea, Fabrizio remained an unsolved mystery. Also, the history museum project as it related to the north-south divide was becoming to some ex-tent political; I decided to take my plight to Joon, the former Korean ambassador to the United States whom I had met at the British enclave.

Joon immediately expressed much-appreciated concern and felt that my pursuers, probably not thugs interested in my handbag, clearly thought I had or knew something of import to them. The days of microfilm were long gone, and since my Cold War years working as an architect at the US Ambassador's Residence in Moscow, I had learned to live life transparently—since we were to assume everything was 'bugged' and we could 'win them over' indirectly through their eavesdropping. So, what were these buffoons after? Certainly not my teaching notes, or plans of the history museum, available online.

If this were a terrorist group, was it enough that I was Christian (as are so many millions of Koreans today), or a professional woman in higher education? Could the intimidation be racially-inspired? My brain continued to search its years of mental archives seeking a rationale. Perhaps this was just a random extremist group and they were singling me out for no more reason than the attack on the tourist bus in Tunis of recent. Perhaps rationality was not what I should be looking for or perhaps, I had just been in the wrong place at the wrong time—but

I instinctively felt there was more involved than happenstance. The year was 2008, and looking back, I think ISIS or Al-Qaida 'sleeper cells' were in existence long before their names became household words—ever since the disintegration of the Turkish Caliphate in 1923 and probably even long before that. But at the time there was certainly nothing to suggest that my Asian pursuers had anything to do with caliphate stirrings except for their use of abayas.

From what I have been able to glean from my student hacker prodigies over the years, it would seem that surveillance operations, ostensibly monitoring 'we the people' more closely than groups like ISIS until they are literally on one's doorstep or 'in your face', cannot compete with terrorist hacking and monitoring techniques or the 'dark web'. I suspected that the email I had sent out before my walk and on-street camera surveillance had been enough to identify my whereabouts to rapidly enable the improvised 'tea ceremony' for whatever reason I was of interest. It was obvious that I would have to be more vigilant, not just with electronic communications but in my 'architectural' walks. Hastily yet thoughtfully I added a whistle, mace, small electric torch, flash drive, and identification tag to my keychain collection, and threw a change of underwear along with my French passport into my bag for any required future rush exoduses. Joon had told me I was welcome to stay with his family anytime, which was of great comfort. He also recommended I go to the police and communicate with my school, which I ultimately did, but as expected, received little reassurance, help or sympathy.

While it seemed unlikely that this event was a random encounter, not knowing what to do I focused on my work and attempted to move on, engaging mainly in 'group tourism' rather than individual promenades. As time passed, I began to think there was perhaps a case of mistaken identity involved, to do with my day-trip to North Korea, or that someone had left or planted something in my flat.

My workaholic response was indubitably a form of denial; I finished another academic article and continued to keep a low profile, watching my back. Construction had started on the Seoul History Museum project, and we were excited by the marvel of 3D reality.

About this time, Christians in Europe and the Middle East had begun to postulate that the anti-Christ of the Bible was likely to be a Muslim extremist, not another European dictator like Hitler, as had previously been hypothesised. Though improbable I marginally explored the possibility that my pursuers might have a connection with the rising caliphate—of which North Korea could be yet another head of a multi-headed hydra. While it seemed far-fetched to think that atheist Kim Jong-Un might be connected to 'extremist Islam', evil has many faces. My brain was having a hard time manipulating the pieces of this puzzle. But I suspected that everything would eventually 'come out in the wash', and that the 'scholars' back at the Cambridge Fellows' House would have some interesting if not enlightening thoughts on the matter. I was anxious to exit Korea.

Two options presented short of returning to Cambridge —a one-year D.Arch. programme in Hawaii, or a teaching stint in North Cyprus (which I did not understand to be so very different from mainstream Europe at the time). Family, friends and budgetary restrictions suggested Cyprus, which promised a fascinating and rewarding experience—it was after all a balmy Mediterranean island. In the end, Cyprus was to prove an invaluable watch-post on Turkey, where Erdogan was building a huge, Fascist-style palace in Ankara more imposing than Versailles—ostensibly as a seat for the next caliph, and for which many contenders besides Erdogan had begun to emerge throughout the Middle East.

•   3   •

Cyprus

IT ALSO MADE SENSE to opt for Cyprus over the one-year 'professional development' D.Arch. Programme at the University of Hawaii (where I had previously taught) as NAAB (the National Architectural Accrediting Board) was scheduled to retroactively revise 3-year terminal professional degree nomenclature from 'M.Arch.' (a degree I held) to 'D.Arch.', although U.S. universities with qualifying programmes were slow to embrace the title upgrade. The new dean was also rumoured to be a bully, and I couldn't see subjecting myself to abuse when I could have that experience at institutions where I'd be handsomely remunerated.

I believe God often puts us where he wants us, when we seek His will, by closing and opening doors that seemingly lie ahead, and at this moment in my life, my 'territory was (ostensibly) being enlarged' to the Mediterranean—as with Sri Lanka, another divided island nation. And the potential for comparative academic research in planning, development, and conflict was enormous.

If corruption is rampant in the developing world, American and European universities are often loaded with back-biting, ferocious academic politics, and one-upmanship, with professors plotting against each other in fierce and almost pathetic competition (over things like parking spaces, trash cans, office size, stylistic language, power plays and teaching schedules)—as opposed to focusing collaboratively on the education and growth of their students and rewarding research projects.

Cyprus was certainly no exception and was to prove dangerous on several fronts.

The first time I noticed something truly amiss on the island was with my students while travelling from Guzelyurt to Nicosia on a field trip; during the 45-minute east-west highway journey between the two small cities my students counted 23 brothels, literally on the highway itself—with others down side roads, and each with a telling name like 'Lipstick', 'Barcode', 'Playboy', etc. Each brothel consisted of a shabby motel structure behind a glitzier main 'disco'/bar building. My students, mostly

Turkish and North Cypriot, explained that the brothels were full of young, mostly Eastern European women who had been trafficked and, everyone agreed, belonged in university instead.

As we considered the enormity of the problem and its implications, I decided to attempt (yet another) architectural 'live project': this time a hostel or halfway house to where such young women might 'escape', find refuge and move on to higher education—a 'bridge back to life'. Two women colleagues at my university agreed to collaborate, and we ran the project in several design studios during the autumn term of 2009. Most of our students took the project very seriously, as did the wife of the then-current North Cypriot president. However, 'sociological background research' was to take us into dark corners of the island where we discovered that many local male students, staff and faculty members from both the North and South sides were frequent visitors to these establishments—as were, possibly, some of my very own students. I have learned that exploitative behaviour, when allowed to run its course, often ends up in severe unhappiness for offenders as well as their victims. The mission at hand was quickly becoming more than architectural and sociological.

It further became evident, through interviews and surveys, that the brothels, as well as the many casinos and some of the dozen or so 'universities' on the island, were interconnected and interdependent, with the schools and casinos serving as money laundering machines—not just for trafficking but for drugs and arms commerce. Since Turkish-occupied North Cyprus is something of a 'no man's land', it is perceived by many as a place where 'anything goes', attracting a plethora of 'misfits'. As we continued to investigate the trafficking phenomenon, communicating with NGO's and religious bodies zealously working to alleviate the plight of these women, we sensed we were becoming a 'thorn in somebody's side'— particularly that of our university administrators, even though, as mentioned, the contested nation's president's wife, a staunch advocate of women's rights, was wholly in favour of our initiative.

Two camps rapidly emerged, and spring semester I was taken off teaching and put on an intensive research agenda which excluded involvement in 'island politics'. Summer term I was shipped off to Canterbury, England to head a fledging satellite design school there. Indubitably other reasons for my transfer besides the attention I had been drawing to trafficking abounded—still, the new venue seemed most definitely related to project focus and my overly high-tech teaching style. My teaching assistant, a Christian Nigerian graduate student who had been promised a scholarship by the university, was dismissed from his job two weeks after the term had started, with no scholarship. This back-handed reneging on promises was to characterise many of my dealings with the Middle East (by the way, Ogah, my TA in Uganda, used to say in private that 'the reason Muslims will not allow churches and the overt practice of Christianity on their turf is because Mohammed cannot compete with Jesus').

While the Koran calls for women to dress modestly, many Middle Eastern and Asian women (including Coptic Christians, Catholics, Hindus and Muslims) traditionally cover their heads in public. In Saudi Arabia, where customary/cultural Muslim dress is carried to an extreme, women react in shock when told the Ko-ran does not require veiling and headscarves (even though they are assumed to have read the book). Many of my Turkish students wore head-scarves, as did some of the North Cypriots (though rarer), and they carried this tradition with them to Canterbury. The North Cypriots themselves generally professed to be 'fed up' with Turkish rule, although they claimed the Turks saved their lives during the 1974 uprising for which they remained grateful—albeit many had not yet been born. Most were resentful of being 'annexed' by Turkey, and Turkish soldiers, friendly enough, were ubiquitous throughout North Cyprus, where the buffer zone remains home to many UN troops today, including the notorious British 'BBC'.

Before being 'deported' to Canterbury (ironically a fabulous place in which to find myself), I had spent a year and a half in Cyprus at two different universities in the north as well as having served as a guest critic/professor at several universities in the south. The Turkish teaching routine (emblematic of the Middle East) had been a shock to my system, requiring professors to be on site and in their offices, if not in the class-room or studio, eight hours a day, five days a week. Exterior site visits and meetings were essentially forbidden unless permission was officially obtained, making research problematic and precarious. There was a pervasive spirit of distrust—another indication that something was 'rotten in Denmark'. Finally, according to one of the former vice-chancellors, all the school computers and offices were monitored via 'remote desktop' or similar surveillance technology, adding to the aura of a 'big brother' caliphate.

Unbeknownst to me at the time of my initial hiring, there had just been a school-wide faculty strike, and the administration had responded by firing the entire faculty. Hence, I had been given the responsibility of 120 students rather than the usual 10-15 in one of my studios. Eventually, I left this university thinking that the five-day-a-week on-site schedule was peculiar to that establishment, only to discover it was worse and more rigorously enforced at the second institution I joined and throughout the Levant. In competition with U. Hawaii, the dean at this school was a tough Turkish female 'despot', and I learned that the Turkish system is full of underpaid, over-worked women professors and administrators who seem to enjoy displacing their own maltreatment on underlings and students. Practice was beginning to look more appealing.

To compound the chaos, in Canterbury, I was asked to teach twelve courses per term as opposed to the usual two or three—covering architecture, interior design, and graphic design.

The situation proved untenable, and in order to exit with my life and career intact, I had to call in the local British police and Architects Benevolent Society in London, threatening a lawsuit in UK courts—where North Cypriot/Turkish standards would never hold. To this day our settlement agreement interdicts discussion, and I am forbidden to write about the experience in depth (not to mention that I might end up like Salmon Rushdie). Suffice it to say that the Canterbury school may well harbour a terrorist sleeper cell of some sort in addition to a money-laundering operation and is being watched closely by the UK's Counter-Terrorism Office.

I had taken my students to the stone work-shop and evensong services of Canterbury Cathedral which they seemed to enjoy tremendously, never having had the opportunity to 'go to church' before not realising evensong was 'church' perhaps—let alone admire the Cathedral's stunning Christian art, architecture and sculpture. Imagine taking students to 'church' in Turkey or Saudi Arabia—it could have cost me my life. I went to a morning Communion service at the Cathedral daily which proved to ground me, as well as proffering new friends and untold unexpected resources.

The University of Kent Architecture School also proved munificent, encouraging me to bring students to their lectures and thereby reducing some of the awful pressure of my teaching load. And of course, Cambridge, which we visited together on a field trip, was relatively close, as were my friends, clients and colleagues in London—another escape route which I rarely mentioned to anyone and which I ultimately had to employ.

One day while strolling through Canterbury's historic lanes I distinctly felt I was (again) being followed—though the memory of old Seoul weighed on me I had perhaps been remiss in letting my guard down. Should I duck into the Cathedral and was it a safe place to hide (or as the site of several famous murders would this be 'tempting fate'), I wondered.

What about Starbucks next door or one of the upmarket boutiques or local book store? My mind raced. Then from the direction of my pursuer, I heard my name called. I turned around, reluctantly, to see Adam, our friendly tour guide.

But he was not alone. With him was a woman wearing a black headscarf, partially covering her face. One of my students perhaps? No, I knew my group well, and none of them dressed quite so conservatively. I felt it was definitely becoming time to explore new employment.

Instinctively I yelled towards Adam, 'Hey, nice seeing you, gotta run! Come visit me at school sometime!' and bolted for my life, towards and into the Cathedral, bumping head-long into Archbishop Rowan Williams as I crossed the sanctuary transept. When my pursuers, who had followed me into the church, saw the mishap, they stopped in their tracks and turned around, walking gingerly out of the Gothic minster.

Rowan had seemingly and unwittingly intervened in my imminent demise. I recalled the red neon crosses on the church roof-tops in Seoul—saved again.

I apologised to Rowan and sat down for long prayer. So long that any pursuer would have become immensely bored waiting for me (prayer always works!). I took the back, little-known pathway home through the Cathedral gardens—telling myself I would have to be more cautious. And rapidly find a new job—even MI5 would be tamer it seemed.

It was about this time that professors were notified that accreditation visitors would be arriving from Cyprus. I had already been manipulated into a kind of purdah in Canterbury, although I needed to return to Cyprus to close down my Ottoman-style village house in Bellapais and sell my car. There was no point in subjecting myself any further to the chicaneries of the Levant I had decided—either in Cyprus or Canterbury.

I had been previously warned that the students were not very serious (which I liked to think I was adept at overcoming). But nobody had told me about the spurious academic (if one could call it that) system, where four years of college at the undergraduate level earned one an architect's Licence, and an additional 3-year PhD (in English) earned one a professorship—no building experience required! Nor had I been forewarned in any way about the draconian on-site office hour schedule. It seemed there was no interest in reform or international architectural education whatsoever and I felt the most positive impact I could have at this point was simply to be supportive to some missionary friends who lived near Bellapais.

I expected my return to Cyprus to be clouded with complications, but it was not. My Pegasus flight via

Istanbul was uneventful—it was good to 'get out' of Canterbury in fact. I looked forward to reconnecting with my friends and colleagues on the south side of the island, which included a Harvard satellite programme in Environmental and Public Health with CUT in Limassol. The northerners usually hated it when I went south and vice versa, but this time nobody seemed to mind in the least. Was I finally no longer a pawn in the corridors of power, what they were, worth shadowing? Something had changed. Obsessive control is such that when it's gone one almost misses it—a kind of 'Stock-holm syndrome', or perhaps just disappointment at indifference. In any case, I packed up relatively easily and left a bunch of superfluous possessions with friends and acquaintances, before saying good-bye. In order to move on in my career, I needed to wrap up the Canterbury venue—I remember thinking it amazing how architecturally remarkable places could be so tarnished and rendered so banal, or even dangerous, by people and circumstances.

It was at Ercan airport on my way out of North Cyprus, just when I thought 'the coast was clear', that a new 'escapade' commenced.

I had flown in, some eighteen months earlier, over the spectacular Gobi Desert from Korea—a long but stunning flight, via Istanbul, not knowing what to expect or why exactly I had been 'called in' by my 'higher power'—

possibly something to do with a few individuals, like Ogah.

At the departure gate of the small rural airport, I presented my boarding pass and French passport to the immigration officer.

'Madam,' I heard him say, 'we cannot let you leave the country.' I looked at him in disbelief. Knowing things had been going too smoothly, and knowing that all my papers were in order, I diffidently asked,

'Is there a problem?'

'Would you step aside please?' the official responded.

And an old familiar waiting game began. I took a seat as motioned in an institutional orange plastic chair against an institutional green wall and waited patiently for some sort of questioning or search. I watched my plane leave and continued to wait. When I protested, I was told that the chief would be with me shortly. I waited for another hour or so. Finally, I decided to take matters into my own hands, went to the ladies' room, and while there called a friend and asked her to come to pick me up. I had had a similar experience in Communist Poland years before with a sick husband and baby in tow, and we had had no option but to turn back (sometime after midnight) to explore alternatives. I had remembered that there usually was a creative solution in difficult situations if one thought things through.

Christine, a retired Norwegian nurse I had met at one of the few surviving churches in the Cypriot north, kindly came to collect me straight away. Since I had just packed up my house and sold the car, she kindly put me up in her guest flat for the night while we commiserated about what to do next. We thought a drive across the border to the airport on the south side the next day would be worth a try. I was to use my US passport and Christine would go with me for an ostensible shopping spree. One thing the enemy typically does not count on is the complicity of the church, let alone 'divine intervention' and prayer!

We set out the next morning with my bags tucked away in the boot and out of sight.

Nobody had called or tried to contact me to my knowledge since I had left the airport. The event seemed to be a form of harassment only—the intent of which was unclear. Obviously, somebody or some entity with pull in the government, and very possibly my university, had wanted to thwart my departure for one reason or another, but motives were hard to follow or fathom. The string of events from country to country could hardly be haphazard artless stalking, as in the days of the Soviet era—certainly more had to be involved. While these maddening episodes seemed connected somehow—involving more than intimidation or persecution—I had decided not to lose any sleep solving the riddle.

As Christine and I approached the border, passing through the vast, sun-scorched terracotta plains of North Cyprus, we prayed. Nonchalantly parking the car as required in the lot ahead of the crossing, we headed to the control booth, got our passports stamped, headed back to the car, and drove through with no questions asked. Apart from the efficacy of prayer, things could be so dysfunctional in North Cyprus (and South Cyprus if one recalls the banking fiasco in which many people lost substantial life savings), that our success wasn't all that surprising—but gratitude was nonetheless abundant. Christine took me to the airport in Larnaca where we light-heartedly said our good-byes. Once again, saved through the Cross.

When I got back to Canterbury, the head administrators seemed surprised to see me, their tell-tale disbelief enormously disconcerting. The larger connection still eluded me, and nobody seemed about to enlighten me in any way. The lawyers I had consulted ages ago as part of a fallback plan were costing me a fortune, so I conferred with the legal arm of the local, charitable Citizens Advice Bureau, where two elderly gentlemen equipped me to file a suit on my own. At the threat of a lawsuit my aggressors backed off, and I headed to the south of France for some respite. With each transition, the next open door always came as a God-send, though inevitably incurred some 'vices-caches' or hurdles down the road: the never-ending cycle of spiritual warfare.

$$\bullet \quad 4 \quad \bullet$$

Uganda

IT WAS PERPLEXING TO family and friends that I chose a visiting professorship in Uganda over an associate professorship at Chaminade University back in Honolulu (which I did, however, accept a year later)—and Uganda turned out to be the highlight of my teaching career. Despite all the real and rumoured corruption and a birth rate of seven children per woman—my remarkable architecture students, the extraordinary accessibility to wildlife reserves and breathtaking safaris, and the charming equatorial campus with its pristine gardens and whitewashed bungalows made the experience unforgettable I also had some brilliant, highly creative colleagues who proved that Uganda indeed has a lot going for it.

One of the first major setbacks our design team ran into was when our orphanage client discovered that most of their 'orphans' were not orphans—dissuading financing for construction. The design team, somewhat indifferent to this posturing since corruption and poverty are seen to abound in the region and duplicity, they argued, 'was to be expected', tried to peddle the work to other NGO's with little success.

Some of the team thought our original client had simply run out of energy, funds and interest and needed an excuse to walk out on the project (not the first time I've seen this comportment—some even appropriate funds).

Though we offered to write grant applications and encouraged follow-through, there was little remedy. While often these projects need to 'sit on the back burner' for an interval, we can overestimate the so-called philanthropic client's ability to conclude their role in a development undertaking, despite trustworthy referrals.

Needing another project for the students to work on while the orphanage project 'percolated', we picked up an outdoor plaza/café for the US Embassy in Kampala. Beyond its face value, this initiative facilitated critical communications when Al-Shabaab threatened to carry out a revenge attack in Kampala similar to that on the Nairobi Westgate Mall (my students were the first to pick up the threat from Facebook). None of us were surprised when Al-Shabaab militants were thwarted and arrested in Uganda over a suspected bomb plot (September 2014).

Around this time, the 'Italian ambassador' to North Korea astoundingly showed up again—but as the facilities manager at the US Kampala Embassy! He did not try to avoid me, and we both burst out laughing when we spotted each other. I had always sensed he was friend not foe, though as a precautionary measure I have learned to question just about everyone's agenda ('trust being earned'). Was this a serendipitous encounter or 'God-thing'? Or was I being shadowed by this character, too? Multitudinous possibilities raced through my mind.

We often don't expect the unexpected or count on these kinds of unforeseen encounters enough—in some ways reminiscent of Graham Greene's 'human factor'. Additionally, the world has shrunk tremendously with the Internet and affordable air travel, statistically increasing the probability perhaps of such happenstance—sometimes fortuitous, sometimes embarrassing, sometimes dangerous.

Given the many tribes and languages (over 33) in Uganda, I was often involved in internal disputes and even asked to settle a few, but outside academe I tried to avoid such involvement like the plague, knowing it could lead to serious controversy.

The rampant poverty, most disturbing given the recently discovered oil and extreme corruption among the very rich, was overwhelming. It seems to me that the rich get richer and the poor get poorer because the rich increasingly exploit the poor, with little or no accountability providing a fertile breeding ground for revolution and terrorism.

On one of our safari trips to the 'orphanage' site near the southern border where Congolese refugees were gathering, my students and I had had several noteworthy encounters. One, in particular, occurred at four-star Mweya Lodge where we went to explore the architecture and interiors and take a much-recommended boat trip through the National Park, where the river and its banks were full of hippos, rhinos, water buffalo, fantastic birds, elephants and leopards—a treasure house full of wildlife in an extraordinary natural environment far surpassing any zoo. However, upon returning from our boat trip, we learned that the park was to close in 15 minutes and that there would shortly be no exit until the following morning. It had taken us a good half hour to get from the park entry to Mweya Lodge, and we were perplexed that no one had informed us of this restriction upon our arrival. We went to the hotel reception desk to find alternatives when two figures cloaked in seamless black abayas emerged from the side foyer. It became immediately obvious to me that prompt departure—begging our way out at the access point, was the only solution on the table. My students and colleagues thought the haste uniquely due to the tight closing schedule (and we certainly did not have funds to spend the night at Mweya Lodge), which was of adequate concern to everybody, especially since we had been told that many of the park's wild animals emerged at night making roaming the reserve beyond 7:00 pm extremely dangerous. To complicate matters, violence had erupted at the border. Our driver, initially difficult to locate, finally appeared out of nowhere making haste, and speeding through the park in our rickety school van paying no attention to potholes and rubble, he got us to the admission gate in twenty minutes flat.

But the gate-keepers were not inclined to leniency. When they called the hotel reception desk to confirm our identity, I wondered who was picking up on the other end—we were certainly not getting the impression they were being helpful. Nor were the students helpful though they shared a language in common with the gate attendants, as they were, by then, quite fearful of any problematic involvement, particularly to do with the nearby conflict.

Night had fallen. Though we had made it to the admission gatehouse safely, we weren't so sure a compulsory return trip to the Lodge would go smoothly. We sat in the van in silence, and waited, wondering if we would have to wait all night. Spiritual warfare, poor planning, or a set-up? Had I imagined what I had seen behind the reception desk? Was I becoming Islamophobic? At this point, again, we prayed. About five minutes into our prayer one of the guards came up to the window on the driver's side of the van, said something I didn't understand and waved us on. We had never been so happy to leave a place. Saved again!

Heading back to our safari camp-site, we sang and yelped with joy. There had been a fire at our lodge a few months back, and we had been given a favourable deal on our trendy tents as much of the place was a charred reconstruction site. We decided to lie low the next morning and enjoy a leisurely breakfast before heading out. Everyone slept well, unperturbed by the chimps yakking in the trees.

Later that morning we serendipitously ran into architect Ross Langdon exploring the neighbouring lodge (which he had designed and for which he was monitoring ongoing construction). Had we known Ross was to be killed in a terrorist attack within 18 months of our visit we would have prayed and shared the Gospel with him immediately. We don't always get the opportunity we think we'll have to confirm redemption after a certain amount of 'relation-ship-building'. Very simply, time is running out.

Mr Langdon graciously showed us around his sensitively-designed, eco-friendly safari resort, taking us into the various 'cottages', meticulously explaining his detailing and design intentions behind each, sharing with us impressive sketches, plans, and models.

He would later visit our 'orphanage' site with one of his clients, a possible donor, and give a lecture on his work as well as some guest desk critiques to students at our university. Ross had worked for Zaha Hadid and claimed it had been a nightmare of 'underling' exploitation, rude briefings and sleepless nights. While the lead ('famous') architect in a firm is often (but not always) responsible for the design of a building or a site, there is typically a whole team involved—often overworked, underpaid, and given little credit—an ill the profession, to my view, desperately needs to address. I had had a similar experience at Gwathmey Siegel Architects in New York where I worked as a young architectural designer fresh out of Columbia University—a particularly challenging residency obligation for a woman in an intensely male-dominated field. At university, we would often go two or three nights without sleep, with accidents proliferating in the model shop and on the studio floor, before a project presentation.

Ross' tragedy taught me that we do not know when death will knock—that we have nothing to lose in being prepared through faith in Christ, and that death does not wait for us to make up our minds. Some of us live in denial—seemingly thinking that death is something that happens to others only and that whoever 'has the most when they die wins,' valuing stuff over love when it should be the other way around. In these seemingly pre-apocalyptic days, it is certain that we will only get a limited number of wake-up calls.

While 'making poverty history' may never be accomplished in our lifetimes—certainly an unlikely scenario walking the streets of Kampala—great spiritual wealth (true success) is not beyond our immediate reach. Having lived in, worked on, and designed dream homes and palaces for 'the rich and famous' as well as far more modest structures in disaster-relief and impoverished arenas, I have learned that true joy comes from relationship—starting with a personal relationship with Jesus, who alone fills the 'soul hole'. Satan's battle for headship takes many forms, from Joseph Kony, Idi Amin, Hitler or ISIS (the 'many-headed hydra')—and to deny the battle or fail to understand where it is coming from can be a form of blindness, folly or indifference.

I have also learned that fighting evil with ignorance or 'Harry Potter-style' wizardry does not, in reality, work.

Only goodness and love overcome evil, and indifference to or tolerance of iniquity make us its active participants, as the Ugandans have so cruelly learned; as Kony's child soldiers are reintegrated into society through conversion and forgiveness, trauma and battle scars recall the nation's very recent toxic past.

Upon returning to the university campus (about two hours southwest of Kampala deep in the bush), I felt it critical to address the question of the black-cloaked figures, so out-of-place at Mweya Lodge. But I didn't know where to begin. Again, I asked myself, who had I managed to pick up and irk so much in my travels and why? Who would have the ability to pursue me so intensely? Did ISIS consider me a target? Did this sort of tracking, persecution and/or intimidation simply 'come with the (spiritual) turf'? And what might be going on electronically or digitally behind the scenes?! Could there be a case of mistaken identity? Should I confront my pursuers? Myriad questions presented themselves with no answers. I decided it was time to consult my colleagues at the US Embassy.

Since the demise of Idi Amin, Uganda has become a largely Christian nation, and the scenario of veiled Muslims working at the four-star reception desk of Mweya was highly improbable.

My colleagues called the Lodge to make a few enquiries, without receiving any helpful response. There was, of course, nothing illegal in what I had seen, and I needed to be careful not to come across as a 'racist' madcap. There had apparently been a similar encounter, however, and that reported by the 'facilities manager' in his travels up north. It was time to find 'Fabrizio', have a serious conversation and connect the dots.

I learned that Fabrizio's real name was Howard and that he was a bilingual Italian-American. As we sipped our coffees in one of the outdoor cafés of the expansive (and expensive) Serena Hotel, he began to explain his role in Korea. Apparently, he had needed to distance himself from the United States for a field operation he was involved in for the U.S. military there.

If he were to be caught or detained for any reason, he was to identify himself as Italian, so that if and when the North Korean Government contacted the Italian Embassy in Seoul, the embassy would honestly have no knowledge of him. His narrative did not yet make much sense.

Our brush with the North Korean authorities had been a close call for Howard. And the North Koreans may have known more than they let on when they chose to 'detain' him.

Though the planet has become 'flat', that Howard was to 'serendipitously' show up again in Uganda was none-the-less disconcerting to me, as was his reported similar encounter with female 'Islamists' in Jaffna, which would not be so unusual. He was not a likely candidate for trust given the history.

I was prepared to listen long and hard however as he continued his story, when suddenly, in the blink of an eye, he jerked back, slumped in his chair and fell forward. I whipped around in the direction of the impact to see a black-cloaked figure behind a column racing towards the entrance lobby—no doubt heading for the glass exit doors. I screamed, and the hotel security guards rushed to us. There had been no sound, no gunshot or other telling noise. One of the guards lifted Howard's head back gently—Howard was clearly dead with a red hole between his eyes. The experience was beyond terrifying.

Now I knew more was going on than a few 'chance' encounters and I remained in shock for weeks if not months, staying in my apartment with drawn blinds. The inquisition/investigation that followed Howard's murder was exhausting, and many questions remained unanswered. The embassy seemed to quickly put a lid on the affair, which was extremely disturbing, and many people inquired about my business with Howard when I didn't have a clear understanding myself of who he was or the exact nature of our relationship. Additionally, no one from the embassy offered any information in the slightest, and the fact that I am writing about this incident now will no doubt upset some government 'officials'.

I felt like I was beating my head against City Hall in the days and weeks following this peculiar tragedy, which did not make the press (like so much of what goes on in the world I suspect). No one seemed concerned about my safety, and my colleagues and students found the whole scenario unbelievable (as I did, for that matter). Howard appeared to have had no family and few friends. Whatever it was he had been about to relate; our 'rendezvous' was clearly connected to his murder. Those days I moved about increasingly vigilantly, 'watching my back', and rarely alone. I was told more murders are left unaccounted for than we would like to think, particularly in troubled parts of the 'developing world', but I was not consoled or about to put Howard's murder to rest. My nightmare was only just beginning to unfold.

At my flat back on campus (a Ugandan-decorated affair with indigenous art and crafts I had collected around the country), I had no alternative but to go on with my daily routine. I took off one morning for my studio heading down the exterior stair as usual. At the bottom of the stair, smack in the middle of the landing, a dead bird lay with its neck broken—a local form of voodoo, though the university at-large was definitely Catholic Christian. I couldn't help thinking that if academia was tough to navigate in the 'West', it was even more problematic in the 'bush'. I wondered if the gesture was directed towards me specifically or at another resident, how much was spiritual warfare, and how much was, again, routine for the turf. I knew our safari trip, and encounter with Ross Lang-don had inspired jealousy, but voodoo? Perhaps the bird had nothing at all to do with me—there was too much vagary clouding all these events to think logically through what had become a labyrinth of both seemingly related and unrelated bizarre and treacherous incidents.

Meanwhile, architectural work in the studio was progressing satisfactorily, and on schedule, although, as often is the case in 'emerging markets', and given the dearth of instructors, I had been asked to teach far more students and contact hours than was humanly possible.

About this time the tourist visa I had for Uganda was due to expire and receiving little help from the school's HR Department towards its renewal, I thought it expedient to take matters into my own hands and make a run across the border into Tanzania, re-entering with a new stamp in my passport. The border was only two hours away by car, so I set out early one day with a trusted university driver and headed south through Masaka, where I stopped to get some bottled water and cash. As we approached the border, which, apart from the scores of trucks lined up waiting for inspection, was hard to recognise let alone find, I knew immediately that the trip had been something of a cockamamie idea. But law mandated a current visa if not a work permit (which the school was reluctant to process), and I had no better solution at that time than to leave the country and head back.

This particular border had never seen the likes of me, and the locals had a heyday with their strange visitor. Fortunately, the university's perspicacious driver was able to relate to and appease the border officials and about three hours after we crossed into Tanzania (on foot), I was able to cross back with a new visa. Given the chaos and delays, nobody seemed to feel a work visa was necessary or worth bothering with—at that point, I had to agree.

Returning to campus, I found that the school administration was astonished not only by my daring but by my unlikely success—there indubitably were angels protecting me, they said. Despite the dodgy paperwork, voodoo, cloak-and-dagger intrigue, murder, academic jealousy, power outages, erratic internet, sparse laundry facilities, and cramped space, I didn't feel it quite time to leave Uganda, as I knew it was critical to get to the bottom of Howard's saga before any departure. I had been asked to be dean but at the same time felt it would be over-committing to accept the position. So, things remained in a kind of limbo.

As I pursued my 'private investigation', the embassy in Kampala tried hard to placate me, to no avail. While I understood that more was going on than met the eye, I could in no way justify indifference to Howard's death. Again, sometimes we need to confront inequity—the trick is often to distinguish position and status from abuse of power. As with delving into the supernatural, we must learn to differentiate between the forces of light and darkness, a skill which can take time, energy and wisdom.

Apart from the US Embassy, I really didn't know where to begin with my research regarding Howard.

The internet was virtually of no use, and he wasn't listed as 'facilities manager' on the embassy website or elsewhere.

There was no response when I called the phone number, he had given me, and there was no listing for the number on the internet or in local phone books either. I was reaching a dead end every turn I made. However, I did recall and find a photograph I had taken in the tour lounge in Seoul before our departure to North Korea in which Howard (a.k.a. Fabrizio) appeared a few hours before his 'inquisition'. But what to glean from it?

[I publish the photograph here in case anybody can help in Howard's apposite identification. He is the man on the left side of the picture. Please do not hesitate to email me at mj292@cam.ac.uk if you can shed any light into this investigation.]

Much to my chagrin, my colleagues began to think I was obsessively fixated on an improbable occurrence. With time I have learned not to discuss matters 'dear to my heart' too openly or too much, as the response is often discouraging as well as disbelieving.

Hence the academic style of the following articles in fulfilment of my various obligations at Cambridge and other institutions, which have also provided useful 'cover', purposely circumvents these intrigues. Two of my better students were willing assistants with my 'research' in exchange for some help with tuition. They were also highly talented digital draftsmen, and we concurrently got a lot of work done on routine commercial projects. Like many young Ugandans, they were sublime computer hackers, mysteriously downloading their assignments on my home laptop at night, for instance, so that I would uncannily find the work there in the morning. These students 'creatively' hacked into embassy computer files to see what they could discover about Howard (whose last name I intentionally omit). They also enquired about him in person at the embassy reception desk, since they had been working on a design project with him and were rightfully concerned. They seemed to enjoy their detective duties more than architecture— things appeared to move forward quickly.

The first thing my students, Nick and Henry, discovered about Howard was that he was not a facilities manager. The second thing was that all his files were classified, and they would need to crack a programme via the 'dark and deep web' to access this information, which for them posed no problem but might be, as they put it, relatively 'dangerous' if they got caught.

Apparently, the embassy would know the files had been opened, but not by whom. I was beginning to wonder if this amateur 'espionage' was wise. We certainly weren't terrorists but the powers that be might label us as such if they wanted us silenced. Just when I was about to call the whole escapade off, Henry and Nick discovered that Howard had spent two years in the Korean Demilitarised Zone, and three years in the Cypriot Buffer Zone as a UN 'peacekeeper'—information that made me nervous although I wasn't sure why or what to make of the findings. He had also held several top security clearances and there were many files linked to him designated 'Top Secret' which the young men were not able to access. We seemed to be getting in over our heads, and some retreat into architectural work made sense.

The day arrived when Howard's 'replacement' came to visit us at the university on our café plaza project, and as a general class question, Nick asked him outright what had happened to Howard. His replacement paled, saying that Howard's tragic 'accident' was still under investigation and that more information would be released in due course. He mentioned that there were many 'extenuating circumstances' which he could not go into for security reasons and changed the focus to the student design work for the entry garden. Immediately picking up on the new embassy officer's avoidance and knowing without a doubt that Howard had been killed, my students, in many respects, kept me sane.

One of the main difficulties in getting aid to disaster relief zones, refugee camps, and needy areas in the developing world effectively is, again, rampant corruption. While one doesn't want to unwarrantedly 'take inventory', one doesn't want to be indifferent to malevolence, greed, incompetence, and inefficiency either. My students and I had not made further progress in our investigation regarding Howard, and as my contract was coming to an end it was beginning to look like I would have to resume 'enquiries' back at Cambridge—dropping the matter was, of course, unthinkable.

Little did I know then that I would not be getting back to Cambridge for another two years—via Hawaii and Saudi Arabia—tales destined for another tome though the Saudi adventure is described perfunctorily in the latter of the following two articles. The massacre of the 142 Kenyan Christian students at Garissa University is a lingering reminder that things could have been far worse for us in Uganda.

•   4   •

Europe, October 2015

I LEFT THE PORTER'S Lodge directly, and in due course had my bags packed for me and shipped to a remote location deep in the south-west of France, a small village where I remain more-or-less electronically inaccessible, pursuing various research initiatives, which continue to include my investigation around Howard. We are in a war, with entities like ISIS and the imminent re-emergence of a caliphate uniquely challenging—but we are not and will not be defeated as long as we stay the way of the Cross.

When I despair, I remember that all through history the way of truth and love has always won. There have been tyrants

and murderers, and for a time, they can seem invincible, but in the end, they always fall. Think of it always.'
—Mahatma Gandhi

Book II: Howard's Identity Revealed

Book III: The Defeat of the Pursuers

Challenges and Recommendations for 'Visitors' Teaching Design in the Developing World towards Sustainable Equitable Futures: Four Divided Nations

Marga Jann, AIA, RIBA, DPUC, NCARB

Poetic Licence / Architects Without Borders / Chaminade University of Honolulu University of Cambridge Centre of Development Studies / Centre of African Studies

All that is necessary for the triumph of evil is for good men to do nothing. – Edmund Burke

Introduction

The four arenas of architectural and design education explored in this article are Sri Lanka, Korea, Cyprus, and Uganda, each of which graciously welcomed the author's teaching and research for a year or so as Visiting Professor.

The study attempts to pave the way for further exhaustive international exchange and cooperation in the design arts towards long-term poverty reduction and sustainable development. The arts, in particular, have much to glean from indigenous cultures and crafts in informing design, making such exchanges mutually beneficial (in multitudinous directions). Additionally, the developing world now has virtually ubiquitous access to digital technologies (if only through 'cracked' programmes and computer 'hacking' levelling the playing field) enabling information exchange and design exploration at the highest levels, particularly in the fields of affordable housing, education, and health facility planning. While sustainable development in the 'third' world needs nurturing, patterns of globalisation suggest that the cultivation of 'ethical intelligence' also merits utmost, concomitant attention.

A sidelight to this paper is a brief exploration of how the architecture and interior design of these four countries, which have suffered extreme strife and division (through civil war and/or outside intervention), reflect this division—typically through monumental symbolic architecture (e.g. political agendas) or neglect (e.g. poverty imposed through failure to 'toe the line').

The study is aimed at professionals engaged in design education both within and without the developing world who endeavour to foster sustainable, equitable development; a common model involves 'live-project' service-based pedagogy and/or 'incubator' hands-on apprenticeship (experiential education).

Ethical Intelligence

As has been extensively documented, corruption and/or greed along with lack of appropriate and relevant education are generally considered major impediments to equitable development. [5]

It is my argument that appropriate design education should include time management (often involving 'cultural readjustment'), marketing and language skills, and a focus on 'ethical intelligence'; otherwise technical design know-how may serve little towards 'making poverty history' (Oxfam slogan). For the purposes of this paper, 'ethical intelligence' is defined as the intelligence that structures stable and dynamic rules that determine the action of the individual in his environment. It determines his capacity to add value, his influence on the environment and on others and his time management. On the one hand, the rules are stable since they respond to a purpose that is defined by the level of ethics within which the individual acts. On the other hand, the rules are dynamic, because, despite the fact that the individual is at a certain level, he can determine alternative strategies that satisfy the objective he is seeking within that level. Ethics is defined as a set of rules that are functional

---

[5] *Corruption major impediment to advancing development, warn UN officials*
http://www.un.org/apps/news/story.asp?NewsID=33190&Cr=corruption&Cr1 last accessed 28.05.2012

to a situation and to a certain perception of an accepted moral and are supported by a complementary ideology.' [6]

For this author, one of the biggest challenges to teaching in the above four arenas representing diverse levels of 'development' was the relative and varying nature of 'ethical intelligence' encountered.

At the onset, I would immediately like to differentiate ethical intelligence from 'academic politics' ('ferocious because the stakes are so small')[7].

Many academic circles exemplify competitive behaviour among students, staff and faculty which often casts a shadow over the generic 'ethical intelligence' of a place; the manner in which such competitiveness is manifested can reflect individual character and, when extreme, tarnish reputation (cheating, dishonesty, fraud, for instance). Job, status and grade contest (similar to sibling rivalry) takes many forms; while not peculiar to the developing world, a dearth of ethical intelligence, or 'alternative' ethical systems (often categorised as 'culture' or more blatantly as 'corruption'), not only inhibits equitable development but creativity and productivity, so important to sustainable high design.

---

[6]http://www.unicist.org/papers/ontology_ei_en.pdf last accessed 28.05.2012

[7] http://en.wikipedia.org/wiki/Sayre's_law last accessed 28.05.2012

Overview

The instructor's task in a problematic 'developing' milieu, in this author's view, is to instill a sense of ethical intelligence as defined above and the need thereof, disengage from local academic politics, and focus on educating students, re-search, community outreach, the promotion of development initiatives within the context of academe engaging students and faculty alike ('live projects' as a more sustainable use of the university), and the advancement of essential skill sets and collaborative human interaction (team work).

Local staff is often threatened by newcomers (and paid far less—or more); 'coffee' or luncheon invitations, fieldtrips, and book exchanges can often help build bridges.

'Chemistry' issues and personality conflicts are not uncommon; in the developing world singularities like culture shock, climate adaptation, health issues (e.g. dengue, malaria, heat exhaustion, poor diet etc.) superstition (e.g. 'auspicious days', fear of witchcraft), disregard for punctuality (alternative notions of time), and language barriers frequently complicate one's job.

The overseas design teaching experience can be tremendously enriching in manifold ways, particularly for designers who enjoy and appreciate travel with patience, humour, and compassion, great strides can be made towards positively impacting local communities and educational methodologies. In North Cyprus, students systematically did not show up until three weeks after the official start of classes and then expected 'make-up' attention. While these students were not mentally deficient, treating them with kindness (facetiously as if they were) allowed a connection which eventually helped the students to see they were wasting their parents' money and cheating themselves out of the full opportunity offered. Conflict in Sri Lanka resulted in students banning a field trip hours before departure, requiring patience, understanding, and alternative strategising.

Belief in the powers of witchcraft threatened to keep a student in Uganda from participating in a site visit to an area his family considered dangerous (he ended up participating anyway and had a terrific experience).

In Korea language problems created contractual misunderstandings and delays, requiring mediation.

Exposure to the wealth of architectural and natural wonders of these places, along with active student progress, made such frustrations manageable (and it is important to find venues of personal satisfaction and 'downtime' to preserve one's 'mental health' and efficiency); in the end, for every student reached (most cannot afford a 'western' education abroad), the prognosis for 'development' improves.

The Dangers of 'Going Native'

Cultural adjustments can have negative as well as positive results when adaptation involves the acquisition of customs that counter 'ethical intelligence' and hinder development. For instance, adopting the habit of showing up late for class, studio or meetings because that is the local 'cultural norm' defeats the purpose of one's anticipated influence. In some cultures, routine deception and lying (diplomatic 'white lies' so as not to offend, for example) constitute a cultural norm, and picking up this trait can not only be counterproductive but dangerous, as corruption and fraud can follow. Periodic furlough (as with embassy staff)—if only 'mental travelling' through books and film—is advisable, providing it does not become abusive.

Other cultural attributes, such as respect for elders and courtesy salutations rather than getting right to the point (as in the case of Korea and Uganda), are of course well worth adopting. Learning a local language always builds bridges, while bargaining like the 'natives' can be interpreted either as miserliness or savvy. Context is important in assessing 'ethical' and appropriate conduct.

Protocol, Etiquette and Nepotism

Different cultures have different takes on protocol, etiquette and nepotism. In South Africa at present, for instance, polygamy is largely considered acceptable (as in many Islamic countries); witness Zulu President Zuma's four wives. Nepotism and cronyism in Africa are well documented and, in many countries, considered 'the norm'. In North Cyprus, two of my colleagues had their adult children working for them as teaching assistants in the Faculty of Architecture, and contracts were issued which stated that 'employees could not leave the country without the employer's permission'. Since North Cyprus (TRNC) was not officially recognised as a 'country', the general consensus was that 'anything goes'. In South Korea, little work was expected of older professionals. In Sri Lanka, loudspeakers went off at 4:00 in the morning on neighbouring street corners with booming Buddhist chants, waking entire communities. In several of my teaching arenas, computers were monitored via 'Remote Desk-top' with related 'hacking' and/or my office was 'bugged'. So, what does one tolerate and respect while teaching abroad? Where does one draw the line and what should one impart to one's students (some of whom are engaged in rampant 'computer hacking')? Some singularities are difficult to change or impact (e.g. 4:00 am loud-speaker chanting), so it is imperative to find constructive ways of dealing with such day-to-day cultural frustrations to avoid 'throwing in the towel'.

Brief Background

I was a Fulbright professor to Colombo School of Architecture and the University of Moratuwa, Sri Lanka from 2005-2006, taught at Duksung Women's University in Seoul, Korea from 2008-2009, the European University of Lefke and Girne American University in (North/Turkish) Cyprus from 2009-2010, and Uganda Martyrs University, Nkozi, Uganda from 2011-2012, with intermittent teaching stints in Hawaii and England (and as a Cambridge University Wolfson College Visiting Scholar, an Affiliate Member of Cambridge's Centre of African Studies, and a Visiting Scholar to Cambridge University's Centre of Development Studies 2011-2013). Previously I had taught between Stanford University in California and Paris and l'Ecole Nationale des Ponts et Chaussées in Paris for six years while maintaining a private architectural and interior design practice.

I discovered the Fulbright opportunity through http://www.cies.org/, the job in Korea via www.acsa-arch.org the job in Cyprus via www.jobs.ac.uk, and the job in Uganda through a contact made at a conference on architectural education in Turkey (where, as in Turkish North Cyprus, underpaid [relative to the other arenas discussed] academics are expected to work the same year-round 9-5 office day as administrative staff) during the spring of 2009.

Fuelled by the Fulbright, I purposefully sought out teaching jobs abroad to the end of furthering fieldwork and research in the domain of sustainable development and because, like most architects, I loved to travel, screening teaching advertisements more by location than by job description.

Interestingly, I ended up predominantly in 'divided nations' ('dystopias' if you like) where the fragmentary political situations render development particularly challenging.

My background in anthropology and sociology at Swarthmore College whet my appetite for working with diverse peoples and cultures, and teaching has allowed me direct contact with the society and mores of the uncommon, exotic nations I visited—professional practice from an overseas base or foreign service employment would indubitably not have afforded such profound intermingling, and I am most grateful for the posts I was entrusted to, as my experiences were both personally and professionally highly rewarding and formative.

I shall discuss each stint and corresponding findings briefly, make comparisons (potentially spurious as they may be), draw conclusions, and suggest recommendations (both for teaching and development).

I

Sri Lanka

While war has now 'unified' Sri Lanka and 'eliminated' the threat from the Tamil Tigers, enforced 'homogeneity' is not unproblematic. I taught in the south of the island in Colombo but visited the north with Habitat for Humanity, working on tsunami reconstruction (see images of student work below) and flooding research. The exercise was demanding due to the extreme heat, mosquito population (dengue as opposed to malaria being a major risk) and acute poverty, particularly in the north and tsunami camps. Additionally, I volunteered my services to a church group (St. Andrew's Scots Kirk, Colombo) engaged in tsunami rebuilding, which landed me in the field about twice a month.

St. Andrew's picked up some of my student 'live project' housing design work and started building from these designs; occasionally construction had to be delayed a month or more as the future occupants insisted on commencing work on 'auspicious days' only, despite their desperate need for shelter.

Additionally, 'locals' typically modified these designs either to save on cost, simplify construction, or, possibly, to appropriate funds. With all the donations pouring in for post- tsunami dis-aster relief work (forty thousand people lost their lives in just ten minutes in Sri Lanka alone), one had to ask where all the international 'star architects' were.

The Sri Lankan Red Cross alone received over $500,000,000 in aid (which this NGO claimed it was 'saving' for 'long-term developments').

Sri Lankan student work (prototypical disaster relief housing)

Teaching was facilitated through a Sri Lankan friend and former IDBE Cambridge classmate, Eeshani Mahesan, who was lecturing at The Colombo School of Architecture (which she later headed) and invited me to co-teach a studio with her as part of my Fulbright; my 'salary' was covered by the U.S. Government (little did I know that this experience was to start a nomadic 'live projects' teaching interlude or 'gypsy office' heavily dependent on virtual space, academe and high tech). For the six years, I taught 'live project' studios at Stanford (contributing momentum for a later 'd.school'[8]), I worked abroad (in Mexico and Guatemala mostly) from a university home base; now I was working in the field/on site with local staff and students in a local university setting. In some ways, this venue was more challenging, and in other ways, it was easier, with the proximity and local 'know-how' facilitating construction and site supervision. Though studios and classrooms were basic and often not air-conditioned, students were generally hard-working, punctual and industrious despite the sweltering heat, and working on disaster relief projects provided a unifying common, urgent goal.

In Sri Lanka, I visited the major work of Geoffrey Bawa, Chelvadurai Anjalendran (who graciously welcomed me to his home) and other remarkable designers who influence me to this day. The cost of building in Sri Lanka is extremely low relative to other parts of the world, enabling high-end detailing and interior design fantasies like swimming pools in bathrooms, outdoor

---

[8] http://www.stanford.edu/class/cee137/ last accessed 04.06.2012

showers etc., with the up-market design sector among the most high-end I have seen.

Pursuant to my séjour in Sri Lanka I spent a year teaching at Judson University outside Chicago facilitating a live village project (now under construction) for tsunami widows in South India (see www.StudioImpact06.com), a camp centre for underprivileged children in the Bahamas, and later, in conjunction with Duksung and the University of Hawaii, an eco-village for Fiji (currently on the 'back burner').

My experience in Sri Lanka kindled my appreciation for the 'extreme', and it was in South Asia that I learned that funding is only one ingredient for sustainable development, and that, when misappropriated, it can certainly be a deterrent.

'Lace House' (Tsunami housing prototype), by Marga Jann / Poetic Licence

II

Korea

My heart leapt when I saw the ad for the teaching job in Seoul, as I had wanted to get to the 'Far East' since childhood, and the Far East kept its promise. I transferred there from the University of Hawaii, which has a strong focus on the Asia Pacific region, and in this sense was well prepared. In addition, my grandchildren were a quarter Korean, which lent incentive. I first visited Seoul with my eight U. Hawaii D.Arch. students for a week in the autumn of 2007, which opportunely 'paved the way'. Eight interior design students from Duksung Women's University then visited us at U.H. in February 2008 before I started teaching at Duksung in March of that year, with the exchange proving highly successful.

The most important challenge in Korea was indubitably language; though I was informed that my Korean students all spoke English, the level of their English was elementary. So, I was expected to teach 'Design English' as well as Interior Design. Another surprise was the racial homogeneity of Korean society, particularly coming from the multiculturalism and multi-ethnicity of Hawai'i. I was about a head taller than everyone and truly felt like a 'Martian'; with the influx of NGO workers in Sri Lanka after the tsunami, I found the Sri Lankans to be more relaxed with foreigners than the Koreans. At the time of writing, inter-racial and inter-cultural marriages are driven by socio-economic needs with little mainstream understanding by Korean society, and Confucian 'machismo' is often syncretically mixed with the dominant Christian faith. At night one drives through a relentless sea of fluorescent red crosses floating above a plethora of churches—a virtual and welcoming light show.

Yet, another big challenge, for this designer, was the visual disturbance of huge graphics covering most

Korean shop windows from top to bottom in Hangul (otherwise a beautiful, calligraphic script) and the relentless social housing blocks (which are now being designed with more variety and flair). The good news about the housing blocks is that they have largely solved the problem of Seoul's informal settlements. Invitations, while appreciated, typically arrived the day of or even a few hours before an event, and sometimes the confusion and lack of fore-thought equalled that of typical 'laid-back' developing countries. The foreign faculty had an expression for anything which required patience and understanding 'beyond the norm': 'T.I.K.' or 'This is Korea'.

From a design perspective, the manifold historic palaces and residences, 'secret gardens', stunning architectural offices and projects (e.g. Heyri Art Valley[9]), rightly flaunted by my welcoming and gracious Korean colleagues, totally outweighed any exasperating cultural experiences. I readily learned to bow rather than shake hands, show appropriate reserve, and share Korean salutations. Contemporary Korean design and fashion competed with the traditional on every level; one had to learn to interpret Hangul posters to take advantage of some of the most extraordinary fashion shows and

---

[9] www.heryri.net last accessed 04.06.2012

museum exhibits this author has witnessed—information was not readily shared with ex-pats in English.

With my students we tackled several 'live projects'; of most interest perhaps is the Seoul History Museum plaza and interiors (see images below). While the exterior plaza (now built) is somewhat disappointing relative to the design work done, we were pleased with the interior renovation work. The 'live project' concept was new to the university and students, as were 3D animations and direct client contact (in this case with the chief curator), and it was rewarding to introduce new methodologies. As with Sri Lanka, all computer programmes were accessible. Students were exceptionally hard-working, and if anything, due to their troubled history, which is not the focus of this paper, Koreans place an extreme emphasis on higher education, with Korean youth largely being 'over-educated', highly competitive, and enormously creative.

Korean student live project design work: Seoul History Museum Exterior Plaza and Interior Exhibit (Duksung Women's University Interior Design Department)

In 2009 I had the opportunity to visit, but not teach in, North Korea. Having worked and lived in Communist Poland and the Soviet Union, I felt very much 'at home', though in a time warp where faces looked different while the dominant culture felt comparable. Like Sri Lanka, the north was very poor; I saw few cars, omnipresent soldiers, and everyone, wearing similar white and traditional blue clothing, rode bikes. Some shops only had one can in the window; from the architecture, I could have been in Moscow or Warsaw during the 1970s.

Propaganda was everywhere; one dared express only prescribed thoughts and feelings—at the centre of which was the 'dear leader' (a pseudo 'deity')—who saw that everyone had what they needed and who made everyone 'happy'. The experience was 'surreal', and some of my fellow travellers and colleagues were reprimanded for laughing at the political slogans and rehearsed explanations; we were heavily escorted everywhere.

III

Cyprus

Of the four countries briefly reviewed in this article, Cyprus was perhaps the most problematic and challenging to navigate. The animosity between north and south was very pronounced, even among intellectuals and fellow professors. I taught both in the north and the south—primarily in the north, but occasionally as a guest critic at the University of Nicosia, which culturally and academically provided a 'breath of fresh air'. Harvard had opened an Institute for the Environment with the Cyprus University of Technology in Limassol which welcomed me from time to time, and I often crossed the border. While the North was not officially Islamic, a culture of control and surveillance governed daily life as well as academics. Additionally, the originally stunning island was being developed with no thought to sustainable planning or zoning.

Academic politics were pronounced, and my non-negotiable Christian French- American background proved an impediment. Positively impacting development promised to be tricky. The kind Indian engineer and dean who originally hired me navigated the indigenous culture with far savvier than I. And my professional experience and academic credentials, stellar in the 'West', did little for me in the Eastern Mediterranean. Like Korea, students spoke very little English, necessitating heavy reliance on graphic communication, and studio size were enormous. Nevertheless, I managed to bond with my apprentices (if only through patience and humour) and saw some terrific work, despite students' reluctance to show up till three weeks after the start of term. Though the computer in my office did not function, and I lived an hour and a half away, I was asked to turn up daily to occupy this office (which did have a beautiful sea view) from 9 am till 5 pm. Because I worked enormously hard and was used to the freedom western academics enjoy, this request went unheeded, and despite overt faculty concern, my stance was eventually respected. While no built work materialised (except for a slew of imaginative birdhouses), the students enjoyed designing a community centre for the local village and a new architecture school, which received some encouraging press coverage.

After six months of the long commute, I transferred to an institution closer to my village home in Bellapais, and, given the unavoidable, abundant sun in Cyprus, worked on research involving a recreational solar park (and design competition) destined for the 'buffer zone'. The idea was to get the north and south to collaborate on producing sustainable solar energy for the island and beyond in anticipation of the eventual fuel shortage while concurrently providing a huge green area or recreational 'eco-park.' My students primarily worked on a tangential competition for revamping the old Olympic Park in Berlin, which is about as 'live' as things got in North Cyprus—and some of the solutions were remarkable (see below example). Again, academic politics proved 'ferocious' in this arena. But I made good friends throughout the island and enjoyed my stay tremendously, though I soon realised it was not an appropriate long-term base for a professional woman with my profile unless I wanted to be constantly 'hitting my head against City Hall'.

Schindler Competition 2010 Entry, Berlin Olympic Park Rehab, by Kumsal Akdogan

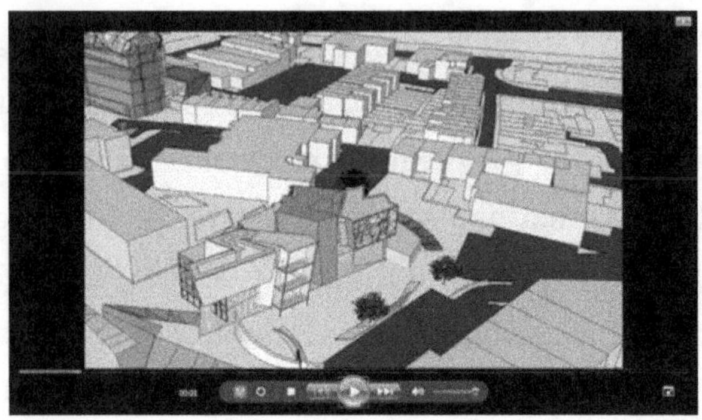

Canterbury Campus Rehab, by Mehmet Cihan Çağal

To conclude, the synopsis of a recent book by Chris Payne is worth quoting, if only for its humour:

Chris Payne writes a hilarious, surreal account of life as a university professor at a dysfunctional university in the Turkish Republic of Northern Cyprus. On the beautiful island of Cyprus, little works as you expect it to, from the primitive plumbing to the maniacal university bus service. The American Institute of Cyprus is a seat of higher learning like no other. The place is chaotically organised for the students who attend class only if they feel like it. They cheat on their exams, photocopy textbooks illicitly with university approval, and deliberately fail their courses to avoid military service.

Meanwhile, the management spends its time devising all sorts of ingenious money-raising scams and schemes to cheat students and teachers alike, while the AIC owner's business strategy is to sell as many university degrees as he can alongside his cake shops and motorcycle franchises. But then, as everyone says, "this is Cyprus," an Edenic Mediterranean paradise where everyone is on the make and the only guiding principle is "money is money." [10]

IV

Uganda

http://www.dipity.com/tickr/Flickr_safari_zebra/

Uganda, from where I write (in conjunction with my Cambridge affiliation), has been an unexpected marvel; the face of Africa is changing rapidly and radically. The Chinese are 'everywhere' working on development projects, much as the West 'infiltrated' China to this end. Little rivals the African 'big game' safari, particularly now

---

[10] Payne, Chris, *Encounters with a Fat Chemist: Teaching at a University in Northern Cyprus,* Author House, 2012 http://www.authorhouse.co.uk/Bookstore/Book-Detail.aspx?BookId=SKU-000575529 last accessed 20.06.2012

that hunting has been banned and eco-tourism is thriving in its stead.

While it is a luxury to have the opportunity to visit first-hand the architectural and urban wonders of our planet, it is quite another to witness 'God's creation' [11]as it was indubitably originally intended; there is simply no comparison between animals in their natural environment and the local zoo.

Africa is perhaps one of the best last places to experience 'divine design', not only in its wild-life but in its extraordinary natural landscape; to my view, it is the designer's high priority and duty to sustainably preserve and respect this 'last frontier'. The downside to this wonder is contrasting extreme poverty, violence and corruption[12], which typify many African countries.

The current birth rate in Uganda, for instance, is seven children per woman (among the highest in the world)[13].

---

[11] Holy Bible, New King James Version, Romans 1:20

[12] Daily Monitor, *Ugandans stash 400b(sh/ $162 m) in secret Swiss banks*, 22 June 2012, pp. 1, 3
http://mobile.monitor.co.ug/News/Ugandans+stash+400b+in+secret+Swiss+banks/-/691252/1432518/-/format/xhtml/-/mlpk2kz/-/index.html
last accessed 22.06.2012

[13]www.ubos.org last accessed 04.06.2012

High-end architecture is rare in Uganda outside the upmarket safari lodge and hotel circuit, though some eco-tourist lodges are architecturally truly remarkable.

My Faculty campus block at Uganda Martyrs University (opened in 1993) was designed by Belgian engineer Firmin Mees; the original Nkozi campus, set in a natural bird sanctuary 'deep in the bush' two hours southwest of Kampala, was a former convent and dates from the 1950s. The grounds are exquisitely maintained, and local architects have designed and constructed additional buildings since which are, to my view, highly commendable (see photos below).

Uganda Martyrs University Main Campus,

Nkozi (Registry Building by Mark Olweny)

Culturally, Uganda has perhaps been as demanding as Korea, particularly regarding notions of time (though they beat those of my North Cyprus students); while Koreans tend to be punctual, notice is often given at the last minute—Ugandans, on the other hand, typically show up late for everything. The level of Ugandan students' English was excellent in comparison (and most Ugandan students speak 2-5 indigenous languages fluently), with four of my first-year students becoming semi-finalists, and a recent graduate a finalist, in 2011.

Berkeley University Annual Essay Competition for Architectural Design Excellence[14].

It is not unusual for family members to be employed by the same employer (as with Stanford University, for instance[15]), and seniority appears to play a major role in local politics. The 'ethical' system seems to be a syncretic mix of 'tribal' culture, current-day international (and often 'unprincipled') business practice, and Judeo-Christian values.

---

[14] Kudos go to teaching assistant Guy Mambo for his initiative in launching and supervising this 'live project'.

[15] http://www.glassdoor.com/Reviews/Employee-Review-Stanford-University-RVW889907.htm, last accessed 04.06.2012

Edirisa Rubona Uganda Martyrs University Orphanage 'live project' at Lake Bunyonyi, Uganda
(Crafts Centre design by UMU student Pam Akora, top right; Nursery School and Library design by students Nicholas Barisigara and Henry Twahirwa, top left and bottom; initial library concept by Joseph Kasimbi)

Taking attendance encouraged students to show up on time, and staggering deadlines helped with meeting deadlines. Climate (relatively cool due to the altitude) and diet have been fairly easy to navigate, with a constant, abundant supply of bananas, avocados, and bottled water delivered weekly. Live projects have included an orphanage at Rubona, Lake Bunyonyi in the southwest of the country (see images of student work above) and a small plaza for the US Embassy in Kampala (under construction, photo below), both of which, though sometimes taxing, have been motivational and educational for students and teaching staff alike. Students had not been using animations, videos or electronic presentations to showcase their work, so a multimedia palette was introduced (which, however, has been slow to catch on).

U.S. Embassy Kampala 'live project' plaza design, FOBE first-year students

Teaching has been done by locals in conjunction with quite a few visiting architects and designers, mostly in rotation, and typically from Australia, Europe or the United States. I was not given a computer, work station or office due to space shortage and my own initial acquiescence, so worked from and held office hours in the housing I had been provided, which I 'redecorated' immediately upon arrival, and where internet access, as well as electricity, proved extremely erratic. This situation, while challenging and somewhat isolating, contrasted vividly to the other extreme of the Turkish North Cypriot modus operandi obliging teaching staff to sit in shared offices daily regardless of school holidays.

The official UMU Faculty office block housed a campus architect's headquarters and private practice/community design service ('in-house consultancy') as well as the usual academic and administrative activities, with boundaries in Uganda somewhat blurred relative to 'Western' notions of 'space planning'. Mobile phones and radios were ubiquitous throughout the country, though there was a pronounced 'digital divide'.

Tangential to any 'dystopia' was a strong Christian spiritual community—the church and religious dimension of the original founding body, whose mission of sustainable service-learning and ethics/good governance pedagogy proved robust and consequential. In the north of the country, for instance, colleagues were very actively engaged in work towards the reintegration of formerly abducted children/child soldiers[16]. While I have not yet been to the north of Uganda, the YouTube video concerning Joseph Kony (largely considered 'ten-years-too-late') has brought substantial attention to the atrocities the region has seen[17]. The scars left by the Amin regime are beginning to heal although corruption remains rampant[18]; this quagmire is being re-visited with the recent discovery of oil (in environmentally-sensitive areas) and through the Inspectorate of Government formed in 1986[19].

Additionally, and promisingly 'Switzerland's Restitution of Illicit Assets Act provides a roadmap for nations who seek Swiss government help in recovering funds that their corrupt leaders stored in Swiss banks' (to date

---

[16] Angucia, Margaret, Broken Citizenship: Formerly abducted children and their social reintegration in northern Uganda, Amsterdam, Rozenberg Publishers, 2010

[17] www.kony2012.com/ last accessed 24.06.2012

[18] *Ugandaanti-graftchieftopressministers' case,* Associated Press, April 13, 2012, http://www.foxnews.com/world/2012/04/13/uganda-anti-graft-chief-to-press-ministers-case/ last accessed 24.06.2012

[19] http://www.igg.go.ug/about/mandate/ last accessed 29.06.2012

Switzerland has acknowledged Ugandan deposits of close to $200m)[20].

The north of the country remains largely ignored and ostracised due to previous political affiliations, and NGO's are still to be found 'everywhere' in the now distant Kony aftermath. There are over thirty-three languages in Uganda, not including the official language, English.

Unyama, northern Uganda
http://www.guardian.co.uk/katine/2008/feb/19/background

---

[20] Daily Monitor, *Ugandans stash 400b(sh/ $162 m) in secret Swiss banks*, 22 June 2012, pp. 1, 3
http://mobile.monitor.co.ug/News/Ugandans+stash+400b+in+secret+Swiss+banks/-/691252/1432518/-/format/xhtml/-/mlpk2kz/-/index.html
last accessed 28.06.2012

Kabale, southern Uganda

http://www.getinvolved.ca/2011/12/49892/

Comparisons

While a few comparisons have already been made, further basic similarities and differences can perhaps be identified between the four teaching contexts (at the same time recognising the dangers of generalisation and bearing in mind the respective 'developing' situations). While each culture requires a specific set of intervention tools, all require patience, humour, compassion, and energy, with background experience undoubtedly advantageous. As mentioned, boundaries of ethical intelligence which allow one to operate without compromising one's moral standards (or moral compass) are wisely established.

While the four cultures I interacted with all demonstrated fairly severe levels of inefficiency, naivety, and inward focus, each had a wealth of indigenous design traditions and customs from which much can be gleaned, and a host of warm, welcoming people. Faculty salaries were rarely paid on time or in a consistent manner, with the exception of the European University of Lefke, North Cyprus and the Fulbright Commission in Sri Lanka. The brothel, gambling/casino and trafficking culture of North Cyprus, indifferent to human rights, was down-right dangerous; sand flies (midges) replaced mosquitoes and carried potential leishmaniasis; water was 'semi-potable'. The low-grade war and Tamil suicide bombings in Sri Lanka while I was there were perhaps less treacherous, while political unrest and overcrowding in Uganda (Kampala especially) warranted vigilance. Korea, apart from North Korea and the attributes already described, was indubitably the most 'developed' of the four 'nations'. In each region, computer programmes, films and music were 'hijacked' (illegally downloaded and copied), with racism on the grounds of appearance or religion fairly extensive (e.g. in Uganda, I was constantly called and identified as a white person or 'muzungu'). When I tried to apply for Sri Lankan citizenship to 'test the system', I was advised that one could apply only if born in Sri Lanka or had a Sri Lankan parent (yet the whole world educates, employs, and naturalises Sri Lankans!).

All four societies were curious and watched me closely, but nowhere was surveillance as rigorous as in North Cyprus, where distrust and resentment (as well as nepotism) were widespread. Upon crossing the border from south to north, one was immediately hit by an onslaught of fake products in shop fronts (e.g. imitation Dior bags etc.). Students typically 'copied and pasted' together papers from the internet (granted English was not the local mother tongue) and were routinely found cheating on exams. Despite the fact that North Cypriots have EU citizenship, the 'limbo' status of the 'Turkish Republic of North Cyprus' (much like the former northern Tamil 'state' in Sri Lanka) ate away at legitimacy in other areas. The 'ethical intelligence' of North Korea needs little discussion.

Most annoying in each arena was the frequent phenomenon of success or achievement being met with jealousy or controversy rather than appreciation (e.g. as a 'hit for the team'); in the 'less developed' milieus students were often more discouraged than encouraged (with negative reinforcement rather than positive reinforcement being the norm), and helping students achieve success did not seem to be high on the academic agenda (one could argue that an 'old-fashioned' teaching methodology remained in place). Finally, many students in the diverse cultures dreamt of 'getting out' beyond just 'seeing the world'—possibly as a result of film and the internet—rather than 'thriving where they were planted' or making things better; most cannot leave (for any substantial period of time) due to financial or political constraints. Development strategies need to exemplify positive change and improvement and produce concrete, meaningful, and visible results or the 'brain drain' phenomenon will indubitably continue to gravely impact all four countries.

Recommendations and Conclusions

International academic exchange in the design arts and architecture is critical to sustainable equitable futures; gleaning information off the world-wide-web is not by itself adequate or as effective as direct contact, and development needs to occur in multitudinous beneficial directions. While sometimes challenging, teaching architecture and design abroad is enormously rewarding provided one stays healthy and does not compromise moral fibre or take oneself too seriously. There is a huge demand for design professors in the 'developing world' warranting further exploration and consideration—particularly in this downturn economy. Many universities are establishing 'extension' or satellite campuses overseas further enabling global outreach (e.g. Harvard in Cyprus, Stanford in Paris, Carnegie Mellon in Qatar).

Apart from the recommendations cited earlier, this author advocates extensive research be-fore travelling, and if possible, an initial exploratory visit to check out living arrangements, faculty facilities, 'local colour', university ethos, and related academic agendas. One needs to have (or develop) a sense of adventure but more and more, even in 'deepest darkest Africa' for instance, one finds familiar products, English spoken, a relative amount of 'creature comfort', internet, mobile phones, and friendly faces. Dialoguing with people from the country one is travelling to on one's home front often dispels fantasies and fears and sitting in on a few classes upon arrival often helps to understand and navigate local expectations and teaching styles. Joining clubs (e.g. chess, film, dance, music, art, book, soccer, choir, etc.) and support and/or church groups can provide a valuable alternative social 'network' and information resource. Some cultures may be too antithetical to one's own moral fabric and in the final analysis, should be avoided no matter how enticing the salary offered.

Finally, expecting the unexpected is part and parcel of any interchange. Deans come and go, coups and wars happen, laws change, friends move on, and our climate has destabilised the world over. Taking one day at a time is the ultimate best counsel and being a 'tourist' wherever one finds oneself—i.e. 'stopping to smell the roses'—lends perspective and critical refreshment. Without balance and boundaries, the overseas educating experience can become draining rather than enriching, with students (and administrators) ubiquitously vying for as much of one's time and energy as they can get. Again, teaching architecture and design in the developing world towards sustainable equitable futures must include a focus on ethical intelligence, marketing and language skills, and time management in addition to standard prescribed pedagogies.

ANNEX

Architecture of Divided Nations

This diversion is the subject of a larger study, but insofar as architecture and design tend to reflect the culture of a people, one can glean much about a place through its buildings and infrastructure—e.g. relative wealth, politics, worldliness, integrity, morals, morale, status, aspirations, and so on—all helpful to the visitor. The most obvious example is perhaps the dilapidated 'Communist-style' architecture of North Korea (what this author sees as reflective of a 'culture of mediocrity') epitomised by the monumental unfinished 'bombshell' of the Ryugyong Hotel in Pyongyang (reflective of a pretentious unworkable political system) compared to the expansive modern (albeit homogeneous) skyscraper development and building in South Korea (e.g. Gangnam, Seoul).

The (unfinished) Ryugyong Hotel, Pyong-yang, North Korea

http://www.instantshift.com/2009/02/19/80-strange-and-fantastic-buildings-architecture/

system) compared to the expansive modern (albeit homogeneous) skyscraper development and building in South Korea (e.g. Gangnam, Seoul). In its way architecture reflects the 'secrets and lies', work ethos, creativity, productivity (or lack thereof) and other attributes of a civilization (e.g. the Great Pyramids of Egypt serve as a testimony to ostensible intense exploitation and cruelty as well as the pharaohs' take on death); it can relate and document stories of division, civil war, conflicting values, and strife—narratives of east versus west, for instance, rich versus poor. And in the divided nations discussed above, architecture documents many sad, sometimes hopeful, and sometimes horrific tales.

The old airport of Nicosia, Cyprus has not been touched since the uprisings of 1974; a plane that never took off still sits on the runway in what is now known as the 'buffer zone' between north and south; driving by one has the uncanny sensation of yet another time warp. Similarly, housing projects in Famagusta decay behind miles of barbed wire; inside, dinner has remained untouched for decades as Greek Cypriots abruptly arose fleeing for their lives and leaving behind everything they owned (as did Turkish Cypriots in the island's south).

Forgiveness is seemingly not on the near horizon, with Greek and Turkish Cypriots alike showing reluctance to move on. The age-old dichotomy is similarly reflected in hybrid or recycled religious structures—cathedrals which have become mosques and mosques which have become churches (see photos below).

Lala Mustafa Pasha Mosque, formerly Saint Nicolas Cathedral, Famagusta, Cyprus

http://www.defence.pk/forums/world-affairs/68865-mosques-around-world-3.html

Selimiye Mosque, formerly Cathedral of St Sophia, Nicosia/Lefkosia, Cyprus

http://www.shutterstock.com/pic-77426677/stock-photo-selimiye-mosque-in-nicosia-formerly-cath-drale-sainte-sophie-nicosia-northern-cyprus.html

Much of the housing in northern Sri Lanka until recently consisted of bombed-out art nouveau buildings such as those in Jaffna or make-shift tents employing large, black plastic 'garbage' bags as the primary building material. Habitat for Humanity has been active throughout the north attempting to restore dignity to survivors of both the tsunami and war.

Evidence of Sri Lanka's indigenous 'star architects' is limited to the south—due to a host of logistical, political, and economic reasons—all hinted at through the island's built form (as with the above example). The siting of religious structures (Buddhist stupas versus Hindu temples) clearly reflects the divide (interestingly, a north-south phenomenon in each of the four countries, with the least 'development' or greater incidence of poverty found in the north).

In Uganda, the thatched huts of the neglected northern hinterland contrast vividly with the more substantial masonry construction boasting corrugated iron roofing of the south (see photos, page 19), where shopping malls and urban congestion abound. Faceless towers reflect Kampala's rapid urban growth, originally dictated by British colonial planning, now revealing extensive haphazard, labyrinthine tessellation. Kampala's Mulago Hospital, initially a gift from the British, lies in functional shambles, a testament to poor maintenance reflecting a sorely lacking sense of ownership.

These examples are but a brief demonstration of architecture's descriptive character. As dress can often disclose the tastes and personality of an individual, so man's larger built habitat testifies to broader issues, such as indifference to the environment, power struggles and turf wars, ideological disagreements and disunion. The architecture of divided nations is one of contrast: heterogeneity rather than homogeneity, dominance versus subjugation, propaganda versus authenticity. As a design educator in the developing world one has the rare opportunity to concurrently visit, observe, and theorise about the local built environment, with students willingly serving as a cultural intermediary. In each country I was able to practice through the design and/or renovation of my own homes and the facilitation of university live projects; I am particularly grateful to the staff and students who made these experiences so rewarding and for the cross-cultural friendships forged.

Episode Two to follow...

BIBLIOGRAPHY

Angucia, Margaret, *Broken Citizenship: Formerly abducted children and their social reintegration in northern Uganda*, Amsterdam, Rozenberg Publishers, 2010.

Ariely, Dan and Gino Francesca, *The Dark Side of Creativity: Original Thinkers Can be More Dishonest, Working Paper*, http://www.hbs.edu/research/pdf/11-064.pdf, Harvard Business School, 2011.

Ayal, Shahar and Gino, Francesca, 'Honest Rationales for Dishonest Behavior' *in The Social Psychology of Morality: Exploring the Causes of Good and Evil*. Washington, DC, M. Mikulincer & P. R. Shaver (Eds.), American Psychological Association, 2011.

Bataille, Georges, *The Accursed Share*, New York, Zone Books, 1988.

Byakutaaga, Shirley Cathy, *Tips on Ugandan Culture. A Visitor's Guide*, Kampala, Fountain Publishers, 2006.

Chugh, D., Bazerman, M., & Banaji, M., 'Bounded ethicality as a psychological barrier to recognizing conflicts of interest'. In D. Moore, D. Cain, G. Loewenstein, & M. Bazerman (Eds.), *Conflict of interest: Challenges and solutions in business, law, medicine, and public policy* (pp. 74-95). New York, Cambridge University Press, 2005.

Easterly, William, *The Elusive Quest for Growth: Economists' Adventures and Misadventures in the Tropics*, Cambridge, Mass.,The MIT Press, 2001.

Fathy, Hassan, *Architecture for the Poor*, Chicago and London, The University of Chicago Press, 1973.

Fouquet, Chantal (Ed.), *Développement durable et architecture responsible: Engagements et retours d'expériences*, Paris, Ordre des Architectes, CNOA, 2007.

Glewwe, Paul and Kremer Michael, 'Schools, Teachers, and Education Outcomes in Developing Countries' *in Handbook on the Economics of Education*, April 2005.

Hayter, Teresa, Aid as Imperialism, Hammondsworth, Penguin, 1971. Hayter, Teresa, *The Creation of World Poverty*, London, Pluto Press, 1981.

Holm, John D. and Malete, Leapetsewe, 'Nine Problems That Hinder Partnerships in Africa,' in *The Chronicle of Higher Education*, Washington D.C., June 13, 2010.

Holy Bible, New King James Version, Nashville, Thomas Nelson Publishers, 1992.

Hutton, John, *Urban Challenge in East Africa*, U. Michigan, East African Pub. House, 1972.

Kanyandago, Peter (Ed.), *The Cries of the Poor in Africa*, Kisubl, Marianum Publishing Co. Ltd., 2002.

Macdonald, John Stuart, 'An Evaluation of Ciudad Guayana, 1965 and 1975,' in *Progress in Planning*, Volume 1, Parts 1 and 2, Oxford, Pergamon Press, 1979, 1-211

Madavo, Callisto, 'Urban Housing in East Africa,' Review in *Canadian Journal of African Studies*, Toronto, Canadian Association of African Studies, Vol. 15, No. 1, 1981.

Narvel, Thomas S. and Lucilla F., *The American Presence in Puerto Rico: Architecture, Planning, Construction*, Working Paper # 78, San German, The Caribbean Institute and Study Center for Latin America, 1998.

Payne, Chris, *Encounters with a Fat Chemist: Teaching at a University in Northern Cyprus*, AuthorHouse, 2012.

Peck, Scott, *People of the Lie*, New York, Touchstone, 1983.

Rice, Andrew, *The Teeth May Smile but the Heart Does Not Forget: Murder and Memory in Uganda*, New York, Metropolitan Books, 2009.

Rodwin, Lloyd and Associates, Planning Ur-ban Growth and Development: *The Experience of the Guayana Program of Venezuela*, Cam-bridge, Mass., The MIT Press, 1969.

Serageldin, Ismail, *The Architecture of Empowerment: People, Shelter and Livable Cities*, London, Academy Editions, 1997.

Sen, Amartya, *Development as Freedom*, New York, Anchor Books, 1999.

Sen, Amartya, *Inequality Reexamined*, New York, Russell Sage Foundation and Cambridge, Mass., Harvard University Press, 1992.

Thurber, Bertha, editor, *Building Community, A Third World Case Book*, London: Habitat International Coalition, 1988.

Lake Bunyonyi, Uganda (Children's Village Site)

MARGA JANN

Architectural Academic Tourism: Saudi Chronicles

or

Social Mobility for Women through Architectural Design and Education in Saudi Arabia

http://www.arabnews.com/node/362096

Marga Jann, RIBA, AIA, Architect DPUC

Visiting Fellow/Research Scholar, University of Cambridge, Lucy Cavendish College Centre of Development Studies / Centre of African Studies
Poetic Licence, Architects Without Borders

THE ARCHITECT: FOUR COUNTRIES FOUR FACES

Taqiyya and Hudna

This paper is a sequel to a monograph about teaching architecture and design in four 'divided nations' (Cyprus, Korea, Uganda, Sri Lanka) and elaborates on a subsequent teaching stint in Saudi Arabia. While KSA is not typically thought of as a 'divided nation', the country and culture, relative to other countries, are in fact (with a few rare exceptions like King Abdullah University of Science and Technology) strictly divided along gender lines. I taught architecture as an associate professor in the Architecture Program of a women's university in the west of the country for the academic year 2013-14 (names are occasionally withheld in this article for reasons of discretion and upon request). While I had taught at a women's college in South Korea (Duksung U), there were ample men on the Korean faculty and access to the campus for men was easy, whereas at the Saudi university, with the exception of one wing which had a few isolated classrooms set aside for 'male' instruction, the attractive interconnected one-building campus was completely exclusionary with tight security.

As a practising architect I had had Saudi clients (and friends) and been to Saudi Arabia before; I saw the stint as a service and research opportunity for and with women in tandem with a Visiting Fellowship at

Cambridge's Lucy Cavendish College, a 'mature' women's college which graciously provided significant moral backing and kind support. Apart from what might seem to the reader to be obvious challenges, the venture was complicated by the fact that the Architecture Program in which I taught went through three program directors that year, was young and had not yet graduated any students, was pursuing draconian Saudi NCAAA accreditation, and though seemingly in denial, was obliged to navigate a growing MERS epidemic (with most cases going unreported)[21]. None of these complications could have been gleaned from the university website or email correspondence with the university before arrival. The ten-year-old college (which was accorded 'university' status in January 2014) was entirely run by women, albeit the Board was composed primarily of men. Many of the women had been hired locally (often Egyptian or Syrian wives of men working in KSA) or by 'local hires' whose understanding of international architectural credentialing was coloured or dictated by that of the Ministry of

---

[21]*MERS: 'A Slowly Growing Epidemic'; Most Cases Unreported*

http://mers-virus.blogspot.co.uk/2013/11/mers- slow-growing-epidemic-most-cases.html last accessed 11 June 2014

Higher Education (MOHE), and substantially different from credentialing and licensing in the UK or US. Architectural licensing procedures modelled on the US system have recently been introduced by the Saudi Umran Society of Architect Registration Council but remain largely ignored.

Complicating academic routine, from this author's perspective, is the Islamic modus operandi of taqiyya and hudna, which accounts for much of what is seen by the expat or 'west' as Saudi or Middle Eastern unreliability or changeability—largely strategic. My delightful Saudi teaching colleagues and assistants would argue that they were subject to the same whims, inconsistencies, teaching over-loads and 'academic politics' as we 'infidels' were, however (of course I was never directly called an 'infidel'). This micro-example means that with Saudization[22] the common perception of employers treating foreign workers like servants is not 'outsider'-specific and has to do with indigenous 'social pecking orders' as well, hinting at yet another potential 'Arab spring'. With the current crisis in Iraq, potential home-grown terrorism, and threatening ISIL caliphate on its

---

[22] Saudization is the national policy of Saudi Arabia to encourage employment of Saudi nationals in the private sector...' en.wikipedia.org/wiki/Saudization last accessed 12 June 2014

doorstep, KSA is currently in a state of high alert (on several fronts). As might be suspected, the model of empowering women in Saudi Arabia through architecture (traditionally a male-dominated field) and design education has not been without trials and frustrations—but the paradigm has proven to have undeniable and profound benefits to all parties beyond the transference of technical skills—lasting friendships, expanded philosophical and psychological horizons, language development, social mobility, increased transparency and accountability, and greater insight into the lot of women in KSA.

Taqiyya ('holy deception') and hudna ('tactical truce') are Koranic principles which basically justify lying or breach of contract (false politesse) to gain the upper hand in dealing with non-Muslims[23]. However, as mentioned, the modus operandi does not seem limited to foreigners and appears to account for substantial in-fighting and confusion among locals as well, with several well-respected Saudi professors/administrators 'let go' by the university in prior years taking the university to court for

---

[23]http://www.inquiryintoislam.com/2010/06/what-is-taqiyya.html, and http://www.thereligionofpeace.com/quran/011-taqiyya.htm last accessed 4 July 2014

breach of contract. It is fairly safe to assume that 'legal' agreements are likely to morph (or be broken) while working in or with Saudi Arabia; in order to survive one has to 'go with the flow', be flexible, exercise patience and diplomacy, expect the unexpected, humour 'upper echelons' and have a good sense of humour. Deception and/or ambiguity might be confused with 'growing pains', yet as one blogger writes, 'the only thing certain in Saudi Arabia is uncertainty.'[24] The university in KSA is not necessarily a safe place to explore/espouse/debate different or opposing ideas or be a 'truth-seeker'/researcher, although my students proved adept at inquiry and felt honesty to be essential. Much has been written about the perils of working in Saudi Arabia as an expat and it is not the purpose of this paper to elaborate on the risks—suffice it to say they exist.

On a positive note in regard to women's rights, King Abdullah is the key player behind the innovative King Abdullah University of Science and Technology, where women can drive, the abaya (typical long black cloak) and head scarf are optional, and classes are co-educational.

---

[24] http://life-in-saudiarabia.blogspot.co.uk/2014/04/procedure-of-final-exit-from-saudi.html#.U7aJofldV8E last accessed 4 July 2014

The university 'has the second largest endowment of any university in the world, second only to Harvard—at $20 billion.[25]'

This remarkable, 'sustainably-designed' campus by HOK Architects has an extraordinary setting and enviable views of the pristine, turquoise blue Red Sea.

Security at KAUST is understandably tight, with the KAUST phenomenon suggesting that KSA leadership is more prepared for a western style of development than the larger population—a position further challenging 'stability'[26].

This upmarket KAUST 'brandscape' is doing much to promote equality for women despite fundamentalist reticence (sometimes, ironically, originating from conservative or 'conditioned' women). Given the background of taqiyya and hudna, and though the 'brand' of Islam practised where I taught, for instance, purported to be one of 'love and peace', 'getting things done' in academe and industry can be problematic.

---

[25] http://www.arabnews.com/news/461379 last accessed 4 July 2014

[26] http://al-shorfa.com/en_GB/articles/meii/features/2009/10/10/feature-02 last accessed 17 July 2014

Women's University, ZFP Architects

KAUST (King Abdullah University of Science and Technology),
HOK Architects

http://www.hoklife.com/tag/kaust/

The Studio or Using Design for Social Change[27]

My architectural studio or lab was constructed as a 'safe place' where 'thinking outside the box' and creativity were encouraged. As one student told me, 'No one thinks like YOU!' Despite occasional cultural differences we were able to make some extraordinary design progress, including live project work for a large garden pho-

---

[27] http://sds.parsons.edu/blog/learn-about-design-thinking-for-social-change/#single last accessed 12 July 2014

to exhibit by and for women, a university fashion show (with the first-ever Fashion Department in KSA), a day care centre for the university, and the UK and US Consulates (in a studio focused on 'culture'). A sampling of these projects is presented below. Animations were explored and created for the first time in the program.

Architecture proved to be not just an end in itself but a medium of expression and haven for what western society considers a highly under-privileged people group (a discussion of how these young Saudi women view themselves is covered in the next section).

As an example of 'cultural misunderstanding,' I was giving a lecture on acoustics when a call to prayer simultaneously sounded. Mentioning 'noise transmission' as potentially disturbing and outlining methods of sound insulation towards more sustainable and user-friendly environments, my commentary was interpreted as insulting by a co-teacher and her attending students, who made an official complaint to the Provost (for the sake of context I should add that my student and peer evaluations were stellar). Studios were spacious and well-furnished though the women lacked designated desk space and storage and could not stay to work beyond 6:00 at night, which during an architectural charrette can be counter-productive.

Live Project Café Pavilion for Photo Exhibit (Razaz Abbas, Marwa Abdulah, Farah Aqrabawi Jinia Sarker)

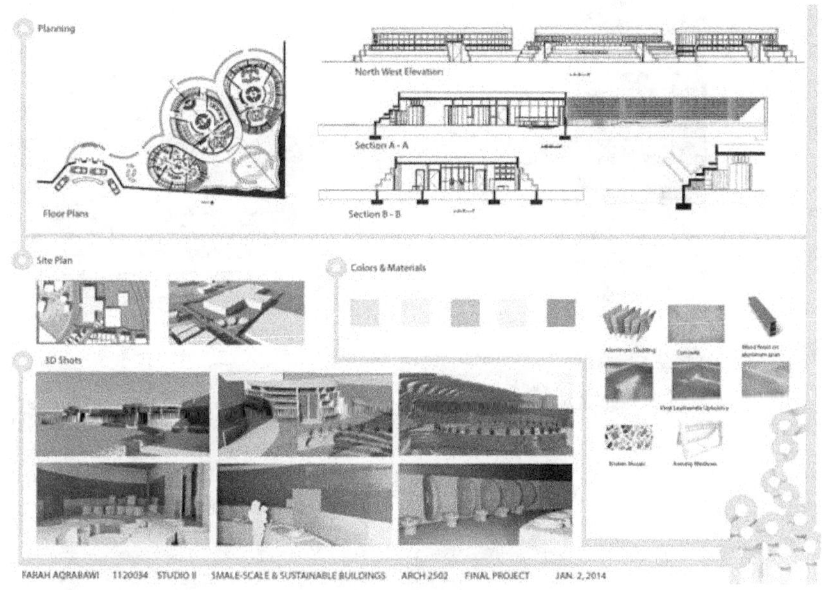

Day Care Centre for Children of Working Mothers (Buthaina Enani, Meaad Hanafi, Rahaf Almuzaini)

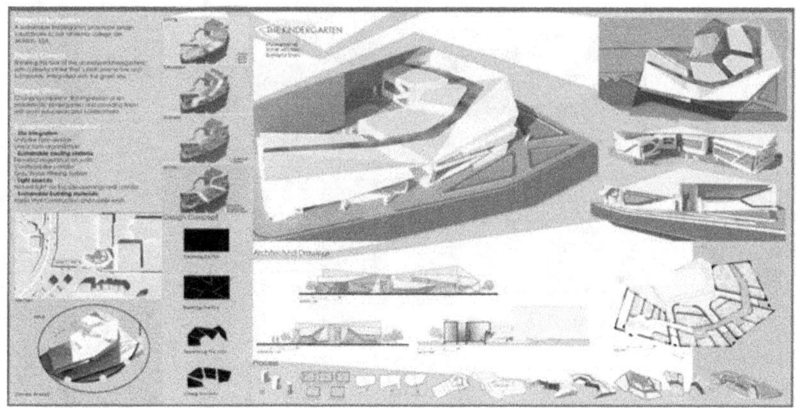

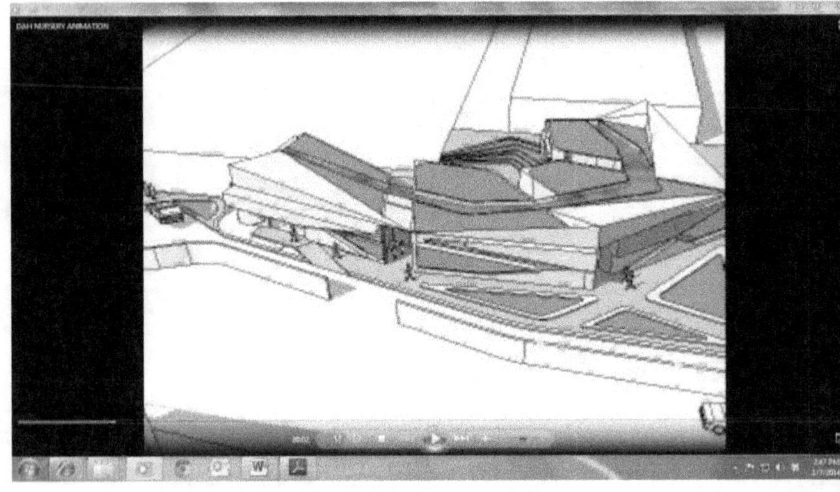

Day care centre video animation

PROF. MARGA JANN
MJANN@DAH.EDU.SA
T.A: SHATHA ABULFARAJ
SBULFARAJ@DAH.EDU.SA
STUDENTS:
TUQA BINLADEN:
TBBINLADEN@DAH.EDU.SA
SAMAHER BAKHSH:
STBAKHSH@DAH.EDU.SA
REMAZ BASRAWI:
RHBASRAWI@DAH.EDU.SA

US & UK Consulate Projects - First Prize Winners

Local Colour

http://www.economist.com/news/international/21601249-designers-are-profiting-muslim-womens-desire-look-good-hijab-couture

While KSA appears very 'black and white' to the outsider and clothing can and typically does reflect culture, it can also be extremely superficial (and is even becoming colourful). The abaya and hijab (headscarf) were not required once inside my university except in the presence of the rare male visitor (as in 'juries'), requiring partitions to be set up in corridors as visual barriers. In the studio, students were 'typical students' although perhaps 'chattier' and more social; many kept their abayas on for the sake of convenience (for the simple reason that lockers were small, cloakrooms unavailable, and air conditioning was kept on high). These young university women did not appear to see themselves as 'handi-capped' or underserved in any way although most felt they should have the right to drive, while concurrently appreciating chauffeured vehicular transportation in navigating chaotic city traffic.

Students told me they could usually go anywhere they wanted with their drivers, although field trip supervision was stringent. When I gave my students a twenty-minute 'free time' break during a field trip early in the year I was called into the direc-tor's office and severely repri-manded (although the students were delighted with the 'liberal approach').

Little information was shared in advance despite nu-merous 'orientation sessions' geared more towards highlighting unforetold and atypical obligations such as daily electronic 'clocking-in' and tedious end-of-term 'course files' (ostensibly required for accreditation). 'Busywork' was abundant.

Most colleagues were in KSA strictly to make money, and most were given substantial teaching overloads since attracting faculty to KSA was difficult despite rela-tively high ('tax-free') salaries. Entry visas could also be problematic. Since interviews were prohibitive due to the complicated visa process, Skype video calls were em-ployed for interviewing, with a colleague remarking that 'mercenaries, misfits and missionaries' were regular re-cruits.[28]

As in Uganda, my students made my time in Saudi truly meaningful and worthwhile, despite any exploitation and competitive faculty under-cutting or rudeness (stemming mostly from insecurity, abuse, jealousy and/or a history of 'women being their own worst enemies').[29]While the school's president held two degrees from Cambridge including a PhD pertaining to the 'Evaluation of Higher Education in Saudi Arabia', the educational system did not, ostensibly, reflect much of the Cambridge paradigm or ethos, which might be expected in a 'developing world' situation and different culture despite forward-thinking intentions. 'Can the Saudi system tolerate hearing the critical voice of a Saudi female researcher and professional?' the scholar asks in her 2005 thesis, reminding the reader of the Islamic shura ('consultation') concept for discourse (as does this author). Saudi men and women alike appear to revert to strict indigenous cultural norms upon returning [30]to

---

[28] http://coa.sagepub.com/content/28/4/406.short last accessed 4 July 2014

[29]http://www.theguardian.com/world/2010/nov/18/women-own-worst-enemies-study last accessed 4 July 2014

[30] [Author's name withheld], *Evaluation of Higher Education in Saudi Arabia…* (U Cambridge PhD Thesis, 2005) page 274

what one expat blogger sarcastically calls 'Paradise,[31]' with the master-servant mentality and pigeon-holing of workers by nationality emerging as a dominant modus operandi (as opposed to collaboration based on competence or merit). One co-worker claimed, 'you have to be mediocre to survive' and another, 'be careful not to upstage your colleagues or you'll be ousted.'

Change and development appear slow, with current norms dictated by government authorities and private university boards/owners, and innovation is typically discouraged (again, KAUST is a welcome exception). Most faculty members have primarily been trained in the Middle East and Africa: Egypt, Syria, Jordan, Turkey, Sudan and so forth, though a good number have spent a few years obtaining a degree in Europe or North America— Muslim colleagues appear adept at learning technical skills abroad without compromising their cultural mores. A remarkable Sudanese lawyer working at my school taught three different legal systems in the Legal Studies Program including Sharia law, managing to

---

[31] http://www.energypost.eu/trouble-oil-paradise-domestic-challenges-saudi-energy-market-global-implications/ last accessed 4 July 2014

compartmentalise the three like languages, with Sharia taking precedence as 'mother tongue'.

Mass email announcements to faculty, staff and students identified university members as 'Dears' or 'Roses', with the president frequently addressing members as 'Darling'. By western standards, students were often overtly/overly affectionate with one another in class, and it is not unusual in KSA for members of the same sex to hold hands (though taboo in public for members of the opposite sex).

At the time of writing, the school is essentially a commuter college open from around 8am-4pm Monday through Friday with a visionary president who has the ostensible where-with-all (and backing) to realise expansionary dreams. My students were eager to learn, though for many (some brides and mothers from a very early age) the experience was more an opportunity to socialise outside the home. During the (ongoing) MERS epidemic, students who had been seriously ill with fever and cough refused to get tested, believing they were more likely to get sicker at the hospital (the only place where testing was available), stigmatised, or quarantined, when little could be done by way of treatment in any case. Only individuals in need of serious help (e.g. mechanical respiration) would actually go to the hospital, and with antibiotics readily available over-the-counter, people self-treated for cough, fever and/or pneumonia.

Typically, no one stayed home to protect others from infection unless they were truly immobile. Since the school required medical certificates from students, staff, and faculty alike in order to officially excuse absences (sick days were otherwise 'docked' from staff and faculty salaries), most everyone showed up despite severe illness, and germs spread easily. In the main students and staff saw western standards of hygiene and quarantine as being 'over the top' and despite mass campaigns to encourage cleanliness, in practice, health concerns were largely ignored. As I often had to spend a half hour or so in close contact with contagious architecture students for 'crits' (individual design critique/teaching sessions) either in the studio or my office, I eventually became quite ill myself. When I asked if I could take a semester off or revert to a more 'western' (flexible) professorial schedule to accommodate research, I was informed that a termination notice would shortly be forthcoming (despite the excellent evaluations from students and peers and a two-year contract). The situation quickly evolved into a settlement by mutual agreement with token extra pay (it should be noted that salaries had diligently been paid on time), with settlement terms broken by the school two weeks later. In the course of a year, my contract had morphed or been reneged on five times without my permission or consultation (taqiyya and hudna).

Though infrequently discussed, students and colleagues alike viewed polygamy and the fact that changing one's religion (apostasy) could result in death (if publicly acknowledged) as highly problematic along with the prohibition of women driving.

Students were awarded prizes for learning the entire Koran by heart, and the initiative was taken very seriously. Some non-Muslim colleagues likened the exercise to 'brainwashing'[32]. At the time of writing, many young women have transformed the abaya into a colourful, loosely worn robe not dissimilar to the kimono or other decorative garb, viewed by some conservatives however as a minor gesture of rebellion ('acceptable in Jeddah but not Riyadh'[33]).

---

[32] http://filmmakermagazine.com/27229-koran-by-heart-director-greg-barker/#.U7aQhPldV8E last accessed 4 July 2014

[33] https://uk.answers.yahoo.com/question/index?qid=20080707085822AABqoTe last accessed 4 July 2014

Due to Saudization and various 'developing world' parameters (although KSA was taken off the EU list of developing nations in 2013), [34]many academic employees are what might be considered to be 'in training'. Hiring is done with little understanding of how various fields and their peculiar dynamics work and differ, particularly at the international level and in the professions—and again, largely due to MOHE directives and the lack of meaningful applicant pools.

At the university I taught at (fairly representative of higher education in KSA in that all universities are governed by MOHE) any degree from Europe or North America was typically seen as an asset while any western licensing processes were generally seen as irrelevant. The

---

[34] http://www.arabnews.com/news/467535 last accessed 4 July 2014

program director's role was apparently to keep faculty 'inline' and grow already oversized and understaffed (and highly unselective) programs (the ubiquitous 'university as commercial enterprise'), rather than focus on appropriate staffing, program improvement and development, sensible scheduling, design excellence and cultivation of team spirit. Bullying and rudeness were not uncommon—perhaps due to 'victims becoming victimisers'[35].

As mentioned, given visa restrictions and the general reputation of KSA regarding women's rights, health issues, freedom of thought and movement, Saudization, etc., recruitment of qualified administrators and faculty was difficult. On the upside, higher education is now available to Saudi women in Saudi Arabia (and the Saudi government provides full scholarships for those wishing to study abroad). While this higher education may be in the 'start-up' phase and a 'work in progress', the machinery is in motion and to be highly commended.

---

[35] http://www.ncbi.nlm.nih.gov/pubmed/10493322 last accessed 4 July 2014

Acculturation

As with 'under-qualification', 'over-qualification' can also have serious drawbacks in any 'developing world' teaching situation and beyond. I was asked to be the acting dean of the School of Design & Architecture shortly after arrival in KSA (a similar opportunity had presented in Uganda) which 'ruffled feathers' even though I was not interested and by MOHE's standards was not a suitable candidate (I am a practising licensed architect rather than the generally preferred PhD in Architectural History or Theory). While students invariably profit from qualified 'expat' instruction and are typically enormously grateful for the contact and input, the teaching mission is severely complicated by academic politics beyond the norm ('ferocious because the stakes are so small')[36], paperwork, and teaching/advising/committee overloading.

Additionally, university women who were victims of polygamy and/or threatened with death for thinking

---

[36] http://en.wikipedia.org/wiki/Sayre's_law last accessed 4 July 2014

outside the system/changing their religion made for disturbed 'bedfellows'.

Navigating culture shock, rivalry and/or frequent exploitation as part of the acculturation process was often handled by expatriate col-leagues through complacency, complicity, silence, 'playing dumb', diplomacy, 'hidden agendas', and/or deception.

The impartation of 'western' values of academic honesty and freedom, creativity, time management, reliability, productivity, tolerance, compassion, responsiveness, work ethics and so forth was by-and-large encouraged and sanctioned in the classroom but not beyond the teaching platform. Many foreign instructors went 'native' fairly quickly, often from fear and to survive KSA emotionally. There are few 'support bases' other than the mosque (although 'house churches' abound and there is an underground Christian movement even among Saudis);[37] one response is to change Islam from the inside.[38]

---

[37] https://www.youtube.com/watch?v=ysfr7rxlT94 and http://www.saudigazette.com.sa/index.cfm?method=home.con&contentid=20140414201838 last accessed 4 July 2014

[38] http://artsbeat.blogs.nytimes.com/2008/05/28/changing-islam-from-the-inside/?_php=true&_type=blogs&_r=0 last accessed 4 July 2014

'Workers' (including women university professors) are normally transported to their employment venues from compounds (or foreign worker housing) [39] daily in school buses at given hours. In my case, the commute was dusty, long and tiring (almost an hour each way), and conversations on the bus were monitored and reported to and by those 'in the system'. Overt and honest discourse could lead to reprimand, ostracism, or dismissal though the bus ride could often accommodate a useful exchange of information between friendly colleagues as well. It did seem that all the walls had eyes and ears. Many colleagues 'escaped' into Red Sea diving, food addiction, Consulate parties, gallery openings, recreational shopping and boyfriends (another KSA 'taboo'). In sum, and as was to be expected, there were substantial complexities and frustrations beyond the norm in connecting with young women in a fundamentalist Muslim venue through the art and science of architecture to improve lives and in-spire/create more positive sustainable environments and futures.

This was not business/teaching or research 'as usual' and acculturation was a tug of war.

---

[39]My 'compound' housing consisted of attractive, air-conditioned, two-storey brick townhouses with seventies' furniture in a tree-lined, architecturally interesting and well landscaped, gated complex with swimming pools, tennis court etc.

An Architecture for and by Women

Several extensive studies have been made about design and accessibility for women-mothers with prams and/or small children and pregnant women, including detailed observations about design issues such as suitable paving for high heels, public bathrooms (usually designed for women by men) lacking counter space, baby changing facilities, hooks for hand-bags and coats, etc.[40] Not surprisingly little has been written about accommodating women in culturally-specific arenas like Saudi Arabia, where dressing rooms in clothing stores do not exist, and public bathrooms do not accommodate ritual washing before prayer (hence women often wash their feet in sinks splashing water all over), hooks for abayas and cloakroom facilities, mechanical ventilation and a choice of western or eastern hygiene, proper floor drainage and so forth. Driving is one of the few instances

---

[40] http://www.architecture.com/Files/RIBAProfessionalServices/Practice/GuidfetoAssistedLiving/AGuideforAssistedLiving.pdf last accessed 4 July 2014

where women are given 'special attention', but in the pe-culiar sense that it has been identified as 'detrimental to women's ovaries'.[41]

Some of the reasoning behind the design or 'architec-ture' of the black abaya and hijab (other than custom)[42] is that the dress provides protection from sandstorms and sun (white, the traditional colour of the men's thobe, would certainly be less heat-absorbent though perhaps more difficult to identify against a desert palette). Some colleagues suggested that given the extensive practice of polygamy (described as 'heart-breaking for any woman anywhere'), the custom of having women cover up pro-vided a welcome impediment to 'wandering eyes', though children lost in supermarkets found it hard to lo-cate their mothers and outsiders found the dress 'frightening' (with 'masking' reminiscent of ISIL). France has gone so far as to ban the face veil, a decision which was recently upheld by the EU.[43] Interesting to note, the

---

[41] http://www.dailymail.co.uk/news/article-2436607/Women-shouldnt-drive-damages-ovaries-pelvis-warns- Saudi-sheikh.html last accessed 4 July 2014

[42] http://www.mwlusa.org/topics/dress/hijab.html last accessed 4 July 2014

[43] http://www.nytimes.com/2014/07/02/world/europe/european-rights-court-upholds-frances-ban-on-full-face-veils.html last accessed 4 July 2014

Koran mentions only the requirement of a loose, modest garment for women (no headscarf or specific colour are called out), whereas the Bible distinctly suggests women 'cover their heads'[44]. Muslim, Christian and Jewish women alike would invariably posit culture and the concept of 'by the spirit not the letter of the law' [45]for their respective interpretations of relevant scripture.

Two live architectural design projects under-taken with my students and colleagues and briefly mentioned earlier, a large outdoor photo exhibit for women by women and a fashion show set for the first ever Fashion Department in KSA, merit some discussion. Further, live projects for the US and UK Consulates were under-taken to give students a glimpse of different cultures and to in-crease self-esteem through working on 'high profile' projects where both men and women government offi-cials sought design input from and listened very carefully to women students. Both the US and UK Consulates hosted exhibits of the student design work (which the young women, however, were forbidden by the school to

---

[44] http://biblehub.com/1_corinthians/11-6.htm and
http://www.mwlusa.org/topics/dress/hijab.html last accessed 4 July 2014
[45] http://en.wikipedia.org/wiki/Letter_and_spirit_of_the_law last ac-cessed 4 July 2014

attend). An introductory small-scale live project included the design and fabrication of a kite (see poster and photos of imaginative student work below).

KITES SHOW

architecture dept 1st (fdsa 1301) & 2nd (arch 2502/3) yr students [northwest and southwest wing corridors now]

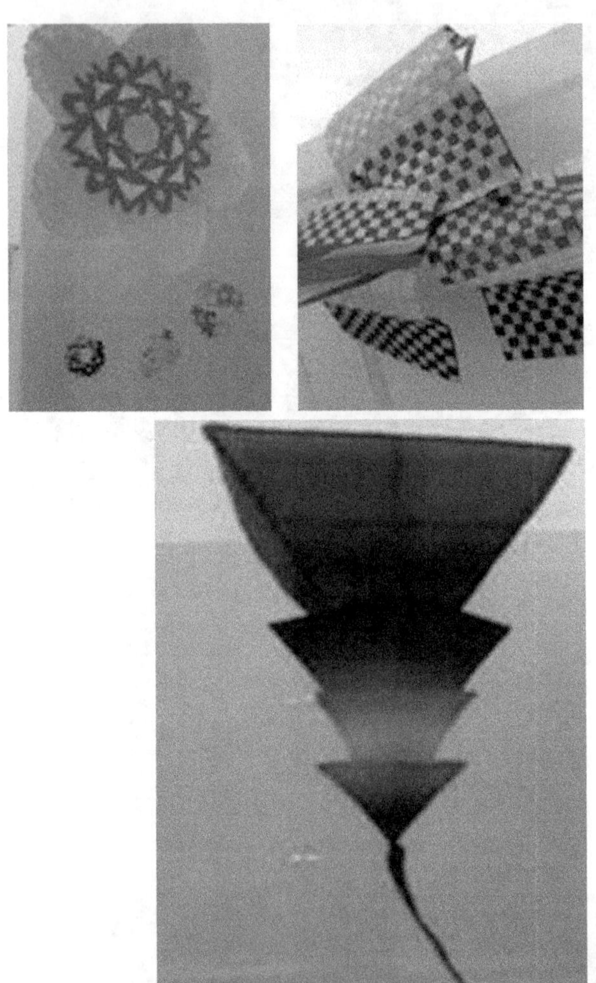

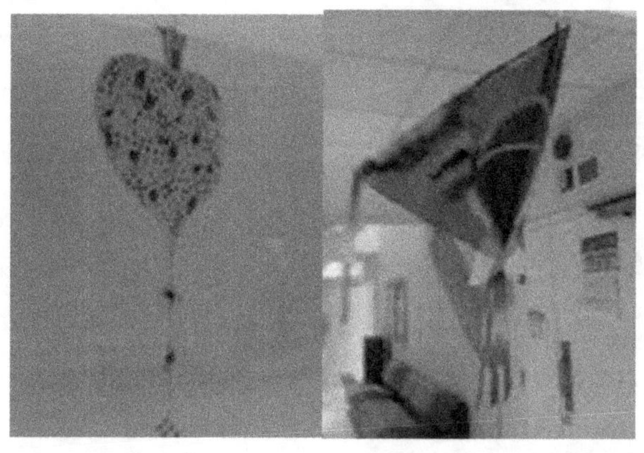

The photo exhibit was the Master's thesis project/brainchild of a school photography lecturer, Zaynab Odunsi, and her mentor, Dr. Effat Abdullah Fadag from King Abdul Aziz University. Zaynab identified and gave training and cameras to ten local women and asked them to shoot an endangered urban neighbourhood, Jeddah's Al Ruwais, in an effort to raise aware-ness about the importance of its preservation and restoration. The initiative was also geared towards the empowerment of the many women involved in the show's production and beyond. Some design work had been done the semester before I arrived, but the site and budget changed dramatically with time and so I was asked to undertake the initiative afresh with my students and younger colleagues. The project was enormously successful, and many students helped with the building of the display pavilions. The below self-explanatory press release offers further insight; numerous articles appeared online and in local newspapers.

FOR IMMEDIATE RELEASE

A Hit for Saudi Women Architecture Students!

In a remarkable pioneering-fashion, women Architecture students from [a Saudi university] have come up with some eco-friendly pavilion designs (which they also helped build) for a photo exhibition by women for women, Hekayat Ashara 10 (http://www.hekayat10.com), this December 2013 in the Jeddah Park Hyatt Hotel gardens. The exhibit was in support of the urban rehabilitation/preservation of a historic district of Jeddah, Al Ruwais, and the students' program was to capture the feel of this neighbourhood and use recycled, recyclable and sustainable materials in showcasing the women photographers' work.

University ARCHITECTURE PROGRAM Studio Critics: Marga Jann, AIA, RIBA, Visiting Fellow U Cambridge, Lucy Cavendish College/CDS (ARCH 2501, 2502), Noor Ragaban (ARCH 2501), Sherin Sameh (ARCH 2502) / Lubna Yasin, Site Manager

Teaching Assistants: Shatha Abualfaraj (ARCH 2501), Yasmin Arslan (ARCH 2501) For further information and names of student designers for each project contact: mj292@cam.ac.uk, marga.jann@gmail.com

A time lapse film was made of the construction pro-cess and numerous web sites emerged from the project. Insofar as the undertaking was not an official university initiative, students felt free to abandon their abayas and enjoy some outdoor seaside 'recreation'.

Building Process (from Time Lapse film by Anggi Makki)

The fashion show set design work might not be exceptional except that it was a first for a fledgling Fashion Design Department in Saudi Arabia. While the MERS 'epidemic' cut the semester short and the project did not come to fruition in the same way that the photo exhibit did, the fashion show did come off—albeit in a large tent in the school parking lot rather than the school atrium for which the sets were designed. One of the student designers (whose project won 'first prize' and is shown below) also modelled in the show. Though photography during the event was not allowed, the accompanying exhibit was open to the larger community, as was the highly professional, collaborative and well-publicised architecture retrospective held earlier in the spring.

First Prize Fashion Show Set Design - Rawand Al Madani

Glass Runway - Remaz Basrawi

Architecture students exhibit innovative house designs

JEDDAH: HABIB SHAIKH & FADIA JIFFRY HTTP://WWW.ARABNEWS.COM/NEWS/557911 Published —

Saturday 19 April 2014 ARAB NEWS

'Breaking Free'

Education is an undeniable key to freedom for women in restrictive Muslim societies—hence so much fundamentalist resistance to it. With all the construction in the

Middle East, it would indubitably be advantageous for locals to share in some of the enviable design work. Architectural education for women has begun and will undoubtedly continue to grow but not without significant ongoing challenges. Within the 'system', creativity appears to be at odds with the apparent lid on thinking for oneself and 'outside the box,' although remarkable examples of both contemporary and historic Islamic art and architecture abound.

Detail from Alhambra, 889/12th C   Angawi Residence 1980s

Balad, Old Jeddah, 20th Century

King Abdullah Financial District, Riyadh (Metro Station by Hadid)

Louvre Department of Islamic Arts, Paris (by Bellini & Ricciotti Architects)

Architecture, while relatively neutral compared to fields such as theology, public policy, gender studies and so forth, provides, in many respects, an exceptional 'point of contact' for interfaith dialogue, 'bridging the unbridgeable' and reducing east-west tensions and con-flict. In the face of ISIL, design can provide some 'crisis intervention' and common spiritual ground transcend-ing the constraints of man-made religion. It is not an easy connection or one without cost, but once made has limitless possibilities providing oases of freedom in both public and secret 'gardens'.

Finally, while KSA still appears very much a divided and developing nation from the ground and 'in the field', from the air (or leer jet) it is hard to grasp the huge dis-crepancy between rich and poor despite the extraordinary oil wealth. Fear has curbed a substantial manifestation of the discontent in the street, but as stu-dents are well aware, freedom is only a click or two (or text) away.

Addendum

(Email from an Anonymous Colleague, 4 July 2014)

Hi Marga,

You have been busy! I admire your perseverance particularly after such a gruelling 10 months.

I just quickly read through your paper, I'll read it much more thoroughly later. I don't think it's too daring, your main points are of course true, and I might get the relevance of many of the points made [better] if I had read your previous reports.

Because I experienced many of your observations, I wonder would the reader ask how you managed to achieve completing exciting projects with the students particularly as you had so little support from higher management. I think it's worth highlighting the main reason which I believe is due to your practical experience; they simply didn't know what you were doing and then when the projects were finished they either took the credit for the success or just side-lined you....I think it's important to shed some light on the behaviour of the senior management and your observation as to why they do not support the expertise they employ. My observation in that regard is that members of senior management are in most cases alumni and have not experienced working anywhere else even those who did work in another university have no varied work experience, even within Saudi Arabia....

Culturally in Saudi, people in senior positions are revered and not questioned and the expectation of that level of subservience combined with an overwhelming lack of experience of different working environments has cultivated a dictatorship which is easily threatened by experienced professionals. Most western profession als will have a bounty of teaching and working experience and they walk unwittingly into a situation where the majority of employees work in fear of losing their jobs. To reinforce this, the top management respond to unwelcome challenges by removing the experienced voice to silence the debate and send an overwhelming message to the weaker subservient workers that such challenges will not be tolerated.

I have asked most of the women in [my] department why they stay? They have been there years and made no progress professionally; their answer was all the same: where will I go? They do not see themselves as having options, so they put up with [the situation]. Saudi women are controlled they only understand control as a method of management, it will take longer than our lifetime to change that. We women in the west have had the right to vote for 80 years and yet we are still fighting to have our experienced voices heard. The Saudi women cannot even get in a car and go to the corner shop, and yet they pretend they have enough understanding and experience to run a university.

It's all laughable really...it's just a matter of debating and qualifying the observations in the Saudi cultural context because the west has no idea.

[Yours truly...]

(Email from an Anonymous Student, 11 July 2014)

Hi Marga!

When I first opened your article, I did what any other lazy person would do, read a few lines, see [if my project might be] featured and be done with it.

But when I read the first page, I knew I had to finish all of it. It is perfect. The part about the university sending mass emails addressed to "dears" and "roses" always got to me. It annoys the hell out of me, and I am so glad you mentioned it.

Your observation and understanding of this place is spot on. When these people say things about empowering women it is nothing but a big fat lie.
Great article! [Anonymous Student]

(Email from an Anonymous Colleague, 18 July 2014)

Dear Marga

Thank you so much for sending me your article which I really enjoyed. You captured the atmosphere at the University in a well-balanced way, as you say, giving credit where credit is due.

I just wanted to mention some points from my own experience if it helps in any way to shed more light on yours.

1.   The University promotes itself as a premier institution for women in KSA. This impressive marketing campaign is what attracts high calibre international recruits (to be carefully distinguished from many locally hired faculty, detailed below) and indeed attracts students. However, after only one week, I saw faculty were working in an atmosphere of fear: fear of student complaints, fear of being fired. After a month, I saw more issues. Students thought they had a realistic prospect of

passing courses, but they were not adequately prepared or qualified to take these courses. This inevitably led to disappointment on the students' part and sometimes conflict, where the faculty would be routinely blamed for student failure. Suggestions on change and improvement were listened to but nothing was done.

2.   In contrast to the impressive international recruitment campaign, some management are picked from an existing pool of staff and thus without management training skills or experience. Incompetence, whether from PDS or faculty, when it arose, was deftly hidden, whereas new faculty such as myself, who were given no support or guidance and made innocent mistakes as a result, were well-publicised by mainly local-hire (non-Saudi) faculty with, sorry to say, poor English language skills and/or possessing poor grade qualifications. Other mismanagement examples I witnessed were:

- Nepotism
- Faculty treated with disrespect and dis-courtesy by management and a large proportion of students
- Discrepancies between written communication and oral, with emails and minutes of staff meetings not reflecting discussions
- Difference in behaviour in front of Saudis and non-Saudis

- Large classes with over 35 students
- Assigning courses to instructors who expressed that they were very uncomfortable teaching courses of which they have no knowledge or experience then accusing them a few weeks into the course of being 'incompetent' and marking down their evaluation
- Not matching courses with faculty specializations
- No official record keeping or sharing of student complaints in a constructive manner with faculty in order to improve
- Lack of modern teaching resources, faculty collaboration, obsession with Power Point as the only tool

3. Gossip and lack of confidentiality seemed to be "normal". A minority of faculty who are insecure about their jobs proved very effective in initiating smear campaigns against new faculty whom they perceived as a threat. Even students were used as tools to implement their plans of "framing" new faculty--such as gossiping with them and inciting and encouraging them to spy on and complain about new faculty (this links with point 5 below).

4. The University is organised in terms of looking good on paper, such as policies on professional conduct, guidelines for disciplinary offences and implementation of Saudi labour law. However, in reality, this was

ignored, and I was saddened at the way in which internationally recruited faculty with impressive credentials were treated.

5.   There are a number of non-Saudi faculty who are not internationally recruited as they are wives of expats working in Jeddah. In November 2013 labour laws were enforced so that 'house-wives' were no longer permitted to work unless they changed their sponsor from the husband's company to the University. Thus, these ladies have transferred their iqamas [resident permits] to the university without having their qualifications verified by the Saudi Cultural Attaché [or appropriate vetting authority] in their respective countries, as international recruits do.

6.   The University is not at all conservative by Saudi standards. The recorded call to prayer, congregational prayers in the atrium and other 'religious' activities sit uneasily with the culture of the University such as the lack of ethics and morals, loud Western music and dancing events (somewhere participation by faculty is compulsory) to the extent that it is hypocritical.

To summarise, I was very disappointed with my academic experience and what kept me going were some pleasant and professional staff (particularly in the library, finance and HR) and the fact that I knew it would only last for another eight months.

[Yours truly...]

BIBLIOGRAPHY

An-Na'im Abdullahi Ahmed, Islam and the Secular State: Negotiating the Future of Shari`a, President and Fellows of Harvard College, 2010.

Ariely, Dan and Gino Francesca, The Dark Side of Creativity: Original Thinkers Can be More Dishonest, Working Paper, http://www.hbs.edu/research/pdf/11-064.pdf, Harvard Business School, 2011.

Ayal, Shahar and Gino, Francesca, 'Honest Rationales for Dishonest Behavior' in The Social Psychology of Morality: Exploring the Causes of Good and Evil. Washington, DC, M. Mikulincer & P. R. Shaver (Eds.), American Psychological Association, 2011.

Chugh, D., Bazerman, M., & Banaji, M., 'Bounded ethicality as a psychological barrier to recognizing conflicts of interest'. In D. Moore, D. Cain, G. Loewenstein, & M. Bazerman (Eds.), Conflict of interest: Challenges and solutions in business, law, medicine, and public policy (pp. 74-95). New York, Cambridge University Press, 2005.

De Graft-Johnson, Ann and Manley, Sandra and Greed, Clara, 'Why do women leave architecture?' University of the West of England, Bristol, May 2003.

Economist, Designers are profiting from Muslim women's desire to look good, Cairo, Jeddah and Riyadh, 26 April 2014. http://www.economist.com/news/international/21601249-designers-are-profiting-muslim-womens-desire-look-good-hijab-couture (last accessed 4 July 2014)

Fathy, Hassan, Architecture for the Poor, Chicago and London, The University of Chicago Press, 1973.

Foran, Clare, How to Design a City for Women: A fascinating experiment in "gender main-streaming", Atlantic City Lab, 16 September 2013, http://www.citylab.com/commute/2013/09/how-design-city-women/6739/ (last accessed 3 July 2014

Fouquet, Chantal (Ed.), Développement durable et architecture responsable: Engagements et retours d'expériences, Paris, Ordre des Architectes, CNOA, 2007.

Garner, Dianne and Prenti, Linn, A History of Women's Seclusion in the Middle East: The Veil in the Looking Glass, New York, Routledge, 2011.

Glewwe, Paul and Kremer, Michael, 'Schools, Teachers, and Education Outcomes in Developing Countries' in Handbook on the Economics of Education, April 2005.

Hayter, Teresa, Aid as Imperialism, Hammondsworth, Penguin, 1971. Hayter, Teresa, The Creation of World Poverty, London, Pluto Press, 1981.

Holm, John D. and Malete, Leapetsewe, 'Nine Problems That Hinder Partnerships in Africa,' in The Chronicle of Higher Education, Washington D.C., June 13, 2010.

Holy Bible, New King James Version, Nashville, Thomas Nelson Publishers, 1992. Kullack, Tanja (Ed.), Architecture: A Woman's Profession, Berlin, Jovis, 2011.

Malcolm, Moira, Student Architect: a TRUE university horror story, UK, Moira Brown, 2013.

Peck, Scott, People of the Lie, New York, Touchstone, 1983. Penwell, Jaq (Ed.), A Guide for Assisted Living, UK, RIBA, 2011.

Sadiqi, Fatma and Ennaji, Moha (Eds.), Women in the Middle East and North Africa: Agents of Change, Oxon, Routledge, 2011.

Serageldin, Ismail, The Architecture of Empowerment: People, Shelter and Livable Cities, London, Academy Editions, 1997.

Sen, Amartya, Development as Freedom, New York, Anchor Books, 1999.

Sen, Amartya, Inequality Reexamined, New York, Russell Sage Foundation and Cambridge, Mass., Harvard University Press, 1992.

Thurber, Bertha (Ed.), Building Community, A Third World Case Book, London: Habitat International Coalition, 1988.

Warah, Rasna (Ed.), Missionaries, Mercenaries and Misfits: an anthology, Milton Keynes, Author House, July 2008.

Weiss, Barbara, Women in Architecture, in The Architects' Journal, 10 January 2014.

Vaid, Ibrahim Y., Saudi Women and Entrepreneurship Opportunities in Architecture and Interior Design, Middle East Studies Online Journal- ISSN 2109-9618- Issue n°6, Volume 3, Summer 2011.

Birdhouse by Shahd Khalil

About the Author

Marga Jann is a French-American architect whose work has appeared in numerous international art and architecture publications. After graduating from Swarthmore College with Honors, Marga Jann obtained her M.Arch from Columbia University Graduate School of Architecture and Planning. At Columbia, she won a Kinne Fellowship for travel abroad and a Lowenfish Prize for the best terminal design project. She was a research scholar at the École Nationale supérieure des Beaux-Arts (ENSBA)-UP6, Paris; holds an MSt in Interdisciplinary Design for the Built Environment (Architecture and

Engineering) from the University of Cambridge and has been the recipient of several Fulbright grants. She is currently a Visiting Research Fellow at the University of Cambridge and works as a licensed, registered architect (Hawaii, New York, and the EU), with her own firm, Poetic License. Marga is also an author, artist, parent, and professor.

Professor Marga Jann is awarded a Senior Fulbright Fellowship to Haiti

last modified Mar 28, 2017, 02:29 PM

The Department of Sociology is pleased to announce that Visiting Research Fellow, Professor Marga Jann, RIBA, AIA has been awarded a Senior Fulbright Fellowship to Haiti (and the French Caribbean), commencing October 2017.

Marga's current research focuses on Urban and Cultural Sociology and Sustainable Design, working within the Department of Sociology, Energy@Cambridge, and Cambridge Big Data. Specifically, Marga's research has concentrated on energy-focused urban and cultural planning issues within cities in the tropics and developing world, examining how shelter and infrastructure can adapt to accommodate mass migration while considering the socio-cultural implications of displacement, homelessness and natural and man-made disasters. Marga is currently exploring and testing smart systems for energy use and regulation in buildings, and lightning as a possible energy generator (in Bolivia).

As a recipient of the Senior Fulbright Fellowship, Marga will be working on post-disaster reconstruction, environmental management and socio-cultural implications of planning prerogatives and initiatives-spending time both teaching and researching.

The Fulbright Program is the flagship international educational exchange programme sponsored by the US government and designed to increase mutual understanding between the people of the USA and other countries. Currently, the Fulbright Programme operates in over 160 countries worldwide.

MARGA JANN

*****

Marga Jann, RIBA, AIA, DPUC, NCARB, Cantab.
Principal, Poetic License www.PoeticLicenseIntl.com
Visiting Researcher, Sociology Dept, U Cambridge [Urban/Cultural Sociol-
ogy + Sustainable Design]
Assoc Researcher, Energy@Cambridge [Buildings + Cities/Smart Design],
http://www.energy.cam.ac.uk/directory/mj292@cam.ac.uk/
Millennium Alliance for Humanity and the Biosphere, Stanford U
Architects Without Borders
AFF Member, Centre of African Studies, U Cambridge 2011-15
Visiting Fellow, U Cambridge, Lucy Cavendish College 2013-14
Research Scholar, U Cambridge, Centre of Development Studies 2012-14
Visiting Scholar, U Cambridge, Wolfson College 2011-12
Fellow, Cambridge European Trust
Fulbright Scholar